The Grace of Patti's

Printed in the USA by

WIMMER
The Wimmer Companies
Memphis
1-800-548-2537

About Our Cover

In 1999, we were given the opportunity to purchase the Ridgetop Mall, a quaint shopping area here in Grand Rivers. Mrs. Julia Badger had developed this warm and inviting place over a period of years and one of the things she had done was to build a tiny meditation chapel in the center of her mall. After we bought the Ridgetop Mall, I decided to move the chapel over to our Settlement to anchor Mom and Dad's memorial garden and at the same time, to open up the Ridgetop Mall so people passing on the street have a better idea of what's there. When we moved the chapel, Mrs. Badger brought me this note concerning her chapel. She's an extremely spiritual person and reading this, you will know that.

> Long ago I heard about the "House on the side of the Road" and being a "Friend to Man." Somehow I thought that "House" should have a steeple on it—and little pews inside. I envisioned people dropping in from their busy rush to sit and just breathe—or meditate—or simply enjoy the stillness and the knowing. It would, of course, have to be serene.
>
> Actually, the more I thought about it, I wondered, "—at the side of WHAT road? How many busy roads have we around here?—At the side of WHAT road?"
>
> Finally, the light flashed on!—Not on a ROAD at all! Instead, smack in the middle of everyday life—center of the workplace—that's where it belongs! Make it a little chapel, with steeple, pews, stained glass windows and all! "ALL," of course, meant the serenity, the repose of spirit— an offering of stillness—laying the burdens down—easing the yoke. And so it went.
>
> That you want to wed within these walls—and take with you the sweetness and the knowing—is your compliment to our effort.
>
> Thank-you.
> Julia Badger

Today our chapel is open 24 hours a day, 365 days a year—use it as our gift in God's love and our parents' memory for your personal needs. "May the peace of the Lord be always with you."

When Mom died in November of 1998, it was a blessing because she suffered so with Lou Gehrig's disease. Because of our faith in Heaven, her departure was almost welcomed. It was a very hard time for Dad especially—his partner in life of 54 years was leaving. Ten minutes after Dad held her hand for the last time, and told Mom he'd be OK and she could go, Mom passed away. Dad's health is not the best and he stays at home with the memories of their life together— enjoying his grandchildren and his many life long friends. Michael T. and I wanted the memory of our parents to last long beyond our lives so together we and our brother, Craig, and sister, Roni, and our life partners designed the granite stone with the story of Mom and Dad's life. We did it out of respect for our parents. In this generation, life is often so busy that we forget to pay respect where respect is due. Our parents are part of a passing era, when above all else people stayed together till death parted them. They stayed together in sickness and in health, for richer or for poorer. They created a strong family unit. They lived their lives for us, their family, and this is our small tribute to that wonderful spirit.

It's been three years since I helped write our first cookbook. Then I had Mom helping me. Today, one of my first friends when I moved to Kentucky is helping me with her part—recipes. His name is Curtis Grace and along with his loving wife, Norma, as well as a few of our employees and their families, we have come together to bring our circle of friends something from the heart and for the belly. Our recipes are simple in ingredients and easy enough for anyone to make. Have fun. This "Grace of Patti's" is dedicated to my dad, the patriarch of our family whose story will be told in the pages to follow.

Many new and old friends alike have read and enjoyed our first cookbook. I hope you'll find this one equally as enjoyable to read, especially as a bedtime story. So many people told me they took Miss Patti's Cookbook to bed and said they just couldn't put it down. They read the whole book, cover to cover; or so I've been told. I'm starting this from the beginning of Hamburger Patti's Ice Cream Parlor and telling our story through 1999. My next book will deal with today, the year 2000, and with our future. This time, I'll tell you about many of the people who have made Patti's what it is today and share intimate thoughts and experiences of our travels along life's highway together. We'll also walk through the architectural stages of development with a pictorial history of the evolution of Patti's 1880's Settlement, with a wind up of what the future holds for Patti's. So take a couple of hours, put on some soft music, start a fire, call your dog or cat up to your lap and come wander with me through a colorful family's life history. Hopefully, you'll go to sleep feeling a little better than you did a few hours earlier. Here's my gift to all who read for pure pleasure, which is something my mother did daily.

This Book is Dedicated to:

Sarah Robertson

"who personifies Patti's personality perfectly"

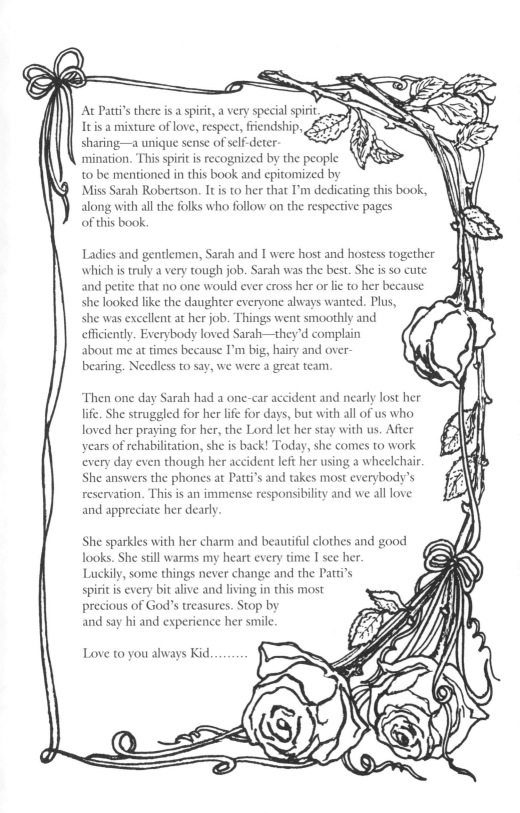

At Patti's there is a spirit, a very special spirit.
It is a mixture of love, respect, friendship,
sharing—a unique sense of self-deter-
mination. This spirit is recognized by the people
to be mentioned in this book and epitomized by
Miss Sarah Robertson. It is to her that I'm dedicating this book,
along with all the folks who follow on the respective pages
of this book.

Ladies and gentlemen, Sarah and I were host and hostess together
which is truly a very tough job. Sarah was the best. She is so cute
and petite that no one would ever cross her or lie to her because
she looked like the daughter everyone always wanted. Plus,
she was excellent at her job. Things went smoothly and
efficiently. Everybody loved Sarah—they'd complain
about me at times because I'm big, hairy and over-
bearing. Needless to say, we were a great team.

Then one day Sarah had a one-car accident and nearly lost her
life. She struggled for her life for days, but with all of us who
loved her praying for her, the Lord let her stay with us. After
years of rehabilitation, she is back! Today, she comes to work
every day even though her accident left her using a wheelchair.
She answers the phones at Patti's and takes most everybody's
reservation. This is an immense responsibility and we all love
and appreciate her dearly.

She sparkles with her charm and beautiful clothes and good
looks. She still warms my heart every time I see her.
Luckily, some things never change and the Patti's
spirit is every bit alive and living in this most
precious of God's treasures. Stop by
and say hi and experience her smile.

Love to you always Kid………

The Lord's Prayer

Our Father, who art in heaven,
    hallowed be thy name;
thy kingdom come, thy will be done,
    on earth as it is in heaven;
give us this day, our daily bread,
    and forgive us our trespasses
        as we forgive those
           who trespass against us;
    and lead us not into temptation,
but deliver us from evil;
for thine is the kingdom,
and the power
    and the glory,
        forever and ever.
        Amen.

Appetizers, Soups and Salads

Our Family

"The Patriarch"

This is a photo of our second dining room at Patti's, the family room so named because it is where the family spent the most time together in the lean early years when there wasn't enough business to keep us hopping. It is also where the family memorabilia seemed to land such as the wall of family photos mixed in with photos of employees and friends. Look and see how much the room changed from 1978 to today.

The next part of this cookbook is about our family, our extended family. In the beginning, I had one older sister and two younger brothers. When Hamburger Patti's started, there were five of us. Then our Patti's family began to grow, including our very first employee, Mrs. Edna Hooks, who now owns and operates the Grand Rivers Fish Market. It seems

after the 3rd year we began to grow exponentially. Today Patti's has 225 employees during high season with a $2,000,000 payroll in a town of 350 people. Patti's is presently the 3rd largest private employer in our county because of the dedication these new members of our family share with each of you, our customers. The stories that follow are from the heart. I wanted some way to record the history of people who were the builders of this company. We've all become family and as with all families, some members are closer than others. I couldn't mention everyone as there have been several thousand individuals over our 24 years who have come and gone but shared in making Patti's what it is today. To those who aren't pictured or mentioned, you are no less a part of "us" than the rest. I only have so many pictures to remind me of everyone. I wish there were more pictures or more room in this book.

Whether mentioned by name or not, you are all Mother's angels. You are what the title is about. I hope I've done you all justice within these pages. And I hope you will tell your family the stories of Patti's like I'm telling our next generations so they will remember the parts each of us played in the development of this company. The picture above hasn't changed since we opened, with the exception of moving this one piece of furniture out to Reflections Gift Shop. It was originally in Mom and Dad's house and the first piece of furniture Mom and Dad bought when they started their life over again in Florida. That one piece of furniture represents our family's new beginning from a dark period.

Mr. William Grant Tullar

Born July 8, 1921 to Mr. Hilton Woods Tullar and Delsa Beyers Tullar. Hilton's parents (my dad's grandparents) were Mr. and Mrs. Grant Colfax Tullar.

Dad was an only child and probably spoiled like the rest of us. As you can see in this picture and so many that follow he's always got something in his hands. Even 70 years ago, he was practicing his puppet repertoire of today.

Artichoke Dip

1   can or jar (6-ounce) artichoke
    hearts mashed and drained
1   cup Hellmann's mayonnaise

1   cup Parmesan cheese
1   teaspoon lemon juice
1   teaspoon garlic powder

Mix all ingredients and put in small shallow baking dish. Bake in 350° oven until top is browned. Serve warm with crackers.

Chunky Artichoke Salsa

1 jar (6.5-ounce) marinated
  artichoke hearts, drained,
  chopped
¼ cup pitted ripe olives, chopped
2 tablespoons red onion, chopped
3 medium plum tomatoes,
  coarsely chopped

1 garlic clove, pressed
2 tablespoons fresh basil leaves,
  snipped
Salt and ground pepper, to taste
Lettuce leaves

Mix artichokes, black olives, and red onion. Add chopped tomatoes, garlic, basil, salt and pepper to artichoke mixture. Mix gently. To serve, spoon salsa into bowl lined with lettuce leaves. Surround with chips or crackers.

Fresh Veggie Pizza Bars

2 cans refrigerated crescent dinner
  rolls (8 ounces each)
2 packages cream cheese, softened
  (8 ounces each)
¼ cup mayonnaise or salad dressing
1 envelope Ranch style Salad
  Dressing mix (1 ounce)
1 medium sweet red pepper,
  chopped

1 medium green pepper, chopped
1 cup grated cheddar cheese
  (4 ounce)
½-1 cup coarsely chopped fresh
  mushrooms, shredded
  carrots, chopped cauliflower
4 green onions, thinly sliced

Unroll dough. Place on lightly greased 15x10-inch pan. Press edges and perforations together to line bottom of pan. Bake at 350° for 7 to 8 minutes or until browned. Cool. Combine cream cheese, mayonnaise and dressing mix. Beat at medium speed until smooth. Spread over crust in pan. Combine peppers and remaining ingredients. Sprinkle over cheese mixture. Cover and chill 8 hours. Cut into 1¼-inch squares.

8 dozen appetizers

Dad graduated from Teaneck High School in Teaneck, NY after majoring in speech and business. Above, Dad is pictured giving one of his first speeches.

Here Dad has Sassy at Mom's parents' ranch outside Tucson in 1944. We children have always had our own pet and I guess it's another trait inherited from our parents.

Calcuttas

12 large prunes	**Major Grey's chutney**
Port wine	**Sliced bacon**

Soak prunes overnight in Port wine. Drain and dry, then remove pits. Fill prunes with chutney. Wrap with bacon and broil until crisp. Stick with pick and serve warm.

Makes 12 appetizers

Below, Dad is standing in front of Mom's parents' (Ronald Fayette Perry & Florence Grundman Perry) house in Tucson, AZ, where all four of us children were born.

Sombrero Spread

½ pound ground beef	1 (8-ounce) can kidney beans
¼ cup onions, chopped	½ cup sharp cheddar cheese, grated
¼ cup ketchup	¼ cup green olives, chopped
1½ teaspoons chili powder	¼ cup onions, chopped
½ teaspoon salt	Tostados or large corn chips

Brown meat and onions. Stir in ketchup, chili powder and salt. Mash in beans with the liquid from the can. Heat well. Serve in a chafing dish. Garnish with cheese, olives and onions. Serve with tostados or large corn chips.

Vegetable Mold

3 large tomatoes, chopped finely
1 large cucumber, chopped
1 large green pepper, chopped
½ onion, chopped
1 pint mayonnaise

1 tablespoon cold water
¼ cup boiling water
1 package Knox unflavored
    gelatin

Mix vegetables and mayonnaise. Add 1 tablespoon cold water to gelatin and stir. Then add ¼ cup boiling water to the gelatin and stir to dissolve. Add gelatin to the vegetable mixture and mix well. Pour into a 2-quart mold and chill until set. Serve with butter flavored crackers or use as a sandwich spread.

After high school, Dad went to work with National City Bank in New York City. He was such an outstanding employee they decided to send him to college at St. Lawrence University in Canton, NY. During the summers he came home to the bank and worked. While in college, Dad learned to fly. World War II broke out during his junior year and he was given six months to join the service of his choice. He joined the Naval Air Corps and enlisted to fly blimps at Lakehurst, NJ. He flew blimps until he developed tuberculosis, which is when and why he was transferred to the veterans' hospital in Tucson, AZ. This is where he met Patricia Ann Perry, my mother.

Cabbage Chowder

2   tablespoons butter
1   pounds Polish sausage
2   cups carrots, sliced
4   teaspoons caraway seeds

2   cans celery soup
1   can milk
1   can water
3   cups cabbage, shredded in long shreds

Cut Polish sausage in thin slices. Brown sausage, carrots and caraway seeds in butter until tender. Mix the soup, milk and water together and add the sausage mix and the cabbage. Bring to a slow boil and simmer ten minutes or until cabbage is tender.

Serves 4 to 6

Cabbage Soup with Cheese

½   pound bacon, chopped
1   onion, chopped
1   bunch green onions, chopped
½   head of cabbage, coarsely chopped
2   potatoes, peeled and diced
5   cups chicken broth
1½ teaspoons mixed herbs (marjoram, savory, thyme, sweet basil and pinch of sage)

Salt and freshly ground pepper to taste
4   ounces Swiss or Jarlsberg cheese, shredded (1 cup)
2   ounces Gouda or sharp cheddar cheese, shredded (½ cup)
¾   cup heavy cream
½   teaspoon dried dill
⅛   teaspoon cayenne pepper

Sauté bacon in a Dutch oven over medium heat until partially crisp. Pour off all but 3 to 4 tablespoons fat. Add chopped onions and cabbage to the pan. Sauté for 5 minutes, or until onions are soft. Stir in potatoes, then chicken broth, herb mixture, salt and pepper. Bring to a boil. Immediately reduce heat and simmer, uncovered, 30 minutes, or until potatoes are tender. Just before serving, slowly add cheeses, stirring until melted. Do Not Allow To Boil. Add remaining ingredients and taste for seasoning.

Serves 6 to 8

Dad, Delsa and Hilton Tullar
(Dad's mother and father), and
Mom

Dad at 19, dressed to kill. From pin stripes to
Hee Haw overalls with a pig on the end
of a leash in one short lifetime........

The Tullar family started with the engagement of
Patricia Ann Perry to William Grant Tullar during the
Christmas holiday season of 1943. Patti and Bill were
married on May 14th, 1944. Dad's roommate's family
and Mom's family were friends when they lived in
Chicago. When the roommate came to visit Dad in
the Veterans' hospital in Tucson, Mom came along.
That is when they first met. To this date, Dad jokes,
"I met my wife in bed." Ha, ha, ha.

A wedding photo of Bill and Patti,
Dad and Mom — May 14, 1944.

Corn and Tomato Chowder

¼ cup chopped celery	1 (16-ounce) can tomatoes
2 tablespoons chopped onion	1¾ teaspoons salt
1 tablespoon chopped green pepper	1 teaspoon sugar
2 tablespoons shortening	¼ teaspoon baking soda
1 (17-ounce) can whole kernel corn	⅛ teaspoon pepper
	3 cups milk, scalded

Sauté celery, onion and green pepper in the shortening until golden brown. Add corn and tomatoes, simmer 5 minutes. Stir in salt, sugar, baking soda and pepper. Gradually stir corn mixture into scalded milk.

Makes about 6 cups

Canadian Cheese Soup

2   medium carrots, cut into 1-inch pieces
2   stalks celery, cut into 1-inch pieces
1   small onion, quartered
2   cups water
2   chicken bouillon cubes
2   cups milk
¼   cup flour
2½ cups cheddar cheese, cubed

Put carrots, onion, water and bouillon cubes into blender container. Cover and process 2 cycles at grind until veggies are finely chopped. Pour into saucepan, cover and cook until veggies are tender. Put milk, flour and cheese into blender. Cover and process, then liquefy until mixture is smooth. Stir into veggie mixture and cook until thickened.

Serves 4 to 6

Cold Strawberry Soup

3   cups fresh strawberries, hulled
¼   cup orange juice
2   cups heavy cream
1   cup plain yogurt
¼-½ cup sugar
½   teaspoon cinnamon
¼   teaspoon nutmeg
½   cup Chambord or other liqueur

Combine the strawberries and orange juice in a blender, process until smooth. Transfer to a large serving bowl and stir in the cream, yogurt, sugar, cinnamon, nutmeg and liqueur. Chill for several hours before serving.

Serves 8 as an appetizer, 4 as an entrée

Curried Broccoli Soup

2 teaspoons olive oil	4 cups chopped broccoli
1 cup chopped onions	1 cup peeled, diced potato
2 teaspoons minced garlic	Salt
1 teaspoon curry powder	Plain nonfat or low-fat yogurt
2 cans low-sodium chicken broth plus enough water to equal 3 cups	

Heat oil in large saucepan over medium heat. Add onions, garlic and curry powder; cover and cook 3 minutes. Stir in remaining ingredients. Bring to boil, cover and simmer until vegetables are tender, 25 minutes. Purée in batches in blender. Season with salt. Spoon into individual bowls. Garnish each with 1 tablespoon yogurt.

Makes 5 cups

Mom and Dad with Roni Lee Tullar (June of 1945) who was named after Mom's father, Ronald Fayette Perry and Mom's brother, our Uncle Ron, whom she loved dearly.

Easy Goulash

1 onion, finely chopped
1 clove garlic, crushed
1 carrot, diced
2 zucchini, diced
1 tablespoon paprika
Pinch of freshly grated nutmeg
2 tablespoons chopped fresh parsley

1 tablespoon tomato paste
1 (14-ounce) can tomatoes
8 ounces cooked kidney beans
⅔ cup tomato juice
Salt and pepper
2 tablespoons sour cream or plain
  yogurt

Fry the onion, garlic, carrot and zucchini in oil for 5 minutes until soft. Stir in the paprika, nutmeg, parsley and tomato paste. Cook for 1 minute. Stir in the tomatoes, beans, tomato juice, salt and pepper. Cover and cook for 15 minutes. Transfer to a warm serving dish. Drizzle the cream or yogurt over the top. Serve warm.

Serves 4

French Onion Soup

1½ pounds onions
⅝ cup butter
1 tablespoon flour
2½ quarts consommé or beef stock
Salt and freshly ground pepper

Slices of toasted French bread
½ cup heavy cream
1½ pounds grated Parmesan or
  Swiss cheese

Slice the onions and sauté slowly in the butter until delicately browned. Add the flour, simmer 2 or 3 minutes, then cook with the consommé and seasonings for 25 minutes. Moisten the toasted slices of French bread with heavy cream. Pour the soup over them, sprinkle the toast with grated cheese and place in the oven or under the broiler to brown. Be sure that the soup does not actually come to a boil.

Serves 8 to 10

Here is a photo of grand-mothers Delsa Tullar (Bill's mother) and Florence Perry (Patti's mother) along with Mrs. Pat Recodray. Our Grandmother Perry lived with us for years while I was growing up after Grandpa Perry passed away and her health deteriorated. Grand-mother Perry (the lady in the dark shorts on the right) loved me more than anything in the world. Un-equally, I should say, compared to my brothers and sister, but I returned her love in kind. We shared a special bond.

While I was growing up, she helped me finance my first business, an adventure at age 14. We lived in a hilly area of Granada Hills, California and I had one paper route. I convinced her and my parents that if they'd let me buy a Yamaha 80 motorcycle, I could have two paper routes and get them done in the same amount of time as one. Grandmother agreed and we bought the bike for $260. I paid her back in six months and was on my way. Thank the Lord the police didn't catch me because I didn't have a license. Grandmother also taught me how to drive in her 1955 Chevy after Dad did some initial training.

Most importantly, she made me study after school. I had a math/science major in high school and had copious amounts of homework. Latin was very difficult for me and Grandmother and I would create flash cards. Then she'd spend hours reviewing them with me. You see, I'm of average intelligence and was even told by a high school counselor to skip college and be happy with trade school. Biology, chemistry and Latin took a lot of work for me. My grand-mother and I loved our time together. She was mostly bed-ridden so this time meant a lot to her and she really is why I was accepted into college and earned my bachelor's degree. In turn, I had to watch Mitch Miller and Lawrence Welk with her. I learned much from her. Later in this book I'll say more—but let me say here that she was the greatest and I loved her very, very much. My dad was special to allow her to stay with us all those years be-cause I know sometimes it wasn't easy to have your mother-in-law living with you.

Nine Bean Soup Mix

1 pound dried red beans
1 pound dried black beans
1 pound dried navy beans
1 pound dried pinto beans
1 pound dried Great Northern beans

1 pound dried split peas
1 pound dried black-eyed peas
1 pound dried lentils
1 pound barley pearls

Combine all beans; mixing well. Divide into 10 packages (2 cups) for gift giving, and present with a Nine Bean Soup recipe. May be stored in a tightly covered glass jar for your own winter soup meals.

10 (2-cup) packages

Nine Bean Soup

2 cups Nine Bean Soup Mix
2 quarts water
1 pound ham, diced
1 large onion, chopped
1 clove garlic, minced

½ teaspoon salt
16 ounces tomatoes, undrained and chopped
1 (10-ounce) can tomatoes and green chiles, undrained

Sort and wash bean mix; place in Dutch oven. Cover with water 2 inches above beans, and soak overnight. Drain beans; add 2 quarts water and next 4 ingredients. Cover and bring to a boil. Reduce heat and simmer 1½ hours or until beans are tender. Add remaining ingredients; simmer 30 minutes, stirring occasionally.

Makes 8 cups

The family in 1958—from the left, Michael, Dad, Roni, Mom, Chip, Craig.

Luscious Parsnip Soup

4 tablespoons butter
1 pound parsnips, peeled and
   thinly sliced
1 cup chopped celery
3 tablespoons flour

¼ cup chopped parsley
⅛ teaspoon white pepper
4 cups chicken broth
Salt to taste
Freshly grated Parmesan cheese

Melt butter in heavy saucepan, stir in parsnips and celery. Cover and cook over medium-low heat for 10 minutes. Place cooked vegetables in a blender with the flour, parsley and white pepper. Add 3 cups of broth and blend at high speed. Return to saucepan and whisk in remaining broth. Simmer over low heat a few more minutes. Serve with sprinkled Parmesan cheese.

Serves 4 to 6

Parsnip Soup

⅓	cup margarine or butter	4½	cups chicken or vegetable stock
1	onion, chopped	1½	teaspoons curry powder
4-5	medium parsnips, chopped		Milk
¼-½	cup all-purpose flour		

Melt the margarine in a saucepan over medium-high heat. Add the onion and parsnips and sauté until tender. Add the flour and stir until well mixed. Slowly add the stock and curry powder. Stir to mix well. Reduce the heat and simmer until thickened. Add milk until the desired consistency is reached. Strain the soup before serving to serve as a consommé.

Serves 6

Special Chicken Potato Soup

2	(10-ounce) cans cream of potato soup	2	(5-ounce) cans chunk white chicken, drained
1	cup water	6	ounces cheddar cheese, shredded
1	cup milk		
2	tablespoons chopped white onion	2	cups cooked white rice

Combine the soup, water, milk and onion in a large saucepan over medium-high heat.

Heat until bubbly, stirring frequently. Add the chicken and cheese and continue to cook until cheese melts. Add the rice; stir to combine and serve immediately.

Serves 6

Here's a wonderful family picture taken at our home in Enchanted Lakes, Kailua, Oahu, Hawaii where we lived from the time I was 9 until I was 12. Notice how we each have animals. All our lives we had pets. I think they are good for children. When you were bad and sent to your room, or if someone made fun of you at school, or life just seemed difficult to bear, you always had your pet who loved you unconditionally. Having a pet could make you never have to feel alone. Having a pet made you feel loved-even when your parents couldn't.

This picture was taken Christmas 1961. Mom received the mirror behind the couch and I got an aquarium. It was probably my favorite present ever, Dad even helped me set it up in the front hallway. I was truly proud of it. When I finished the third floor of my house for my 50th birthday, I bought a fish tank, my first in 40 years. I still love it.

Zesty Mexican Soup

2 cups cubed cooked chicken
1 (14-ounce) can chicken broth
1 (11-ounce) can vegetable juice
   cocktail

1 (11-ounce) can Mexicorn
1 cup salsa
1 (4-ounce) can chopped green
   chiles

Combine the chicken, chicken broth, vegetable juice cocktail, Mexicorn, salsa and green chiles. Bring to boil over medium-high heat. Reduce heat and simmer for 10 minutes.

Serves 6

Here we are (from the left, Chip, Craig, Bill, Patti, Michael, Roni) at the same house outside with Tyla, our champion German shepherd. Mom, while at home, raised Tyla's pups and would sell them. This would pay her way back to the mainland when Dad would take business trips back to California. As you can see, we were, as we still are, a happy bunch.

From the left, Craig, Bill, Patti, Michael.

A couple years later we moved to Granada Hills, California and brought with us a new Mercury Comet on which everyone is leaning in the picture. Well, in Hawaii where no speed limit ever exceeded 45 m.p.h., the gutless wonder Comet was fine, but Dad nearly got us all killed when we moved back to the mainland. When we tried to merge onto a freeway, we had so little acceleration we were dead ducks. It didn't hold up to Los Angeles' pace.

While in Hawaii, the Comet was a huge step up from Mom's 1949 blue beetle, a DeSoto. This poor rattle trap shook violently every time Mom tried to reach the island's 35 m.p.h. speed limit. There were no four lane roads, only single lanes in Hawaii back in the 1950's. The DeSoto would not go over 30 m.p.h.. So when Mom loaded us kids up, surfboards and all, to go to the beach after school, which she did almost daily, we'd have a long line of traffic backed up behind us, the blue beetle leading the way. She was a great Mom and we loved the blue beetle—hated the Comet. At least the blue beetle was a fun car for us.

Cranberry Salad

18 ounces strawberry, cherry or raspberry gelatin

2½ cups orange juice

1 (20-ounce) can of crushed pineapple, not drained

2 cans whole berry cranberry sauce

3 apples, peeled and chopped, dipped in lemon juice

6 oranges, sectioned

2 tablespoons grated orange peel

1½ cups toasted chopped pecans

Dissolve gelatin in boiling orange juice. Add cranberry sauce to hot gelatin. Add pineapple, apple, oranges, grated orange peel and nuts. Allow to congeal slightly then pour into mold which has been lightly greased with mayonnaise or vegetable spray. Refrigerate to congeal.

Serves 18

Banana Salad

1 tablespoon lemon juice

2 tablespoons mayonnaise

6 ounces cream cheese

1 small can crushed pineapple

½ cup maraschino cherries, cut

½ cup nuts

1 cup heavy cream, whipped

3 ripe bananas

1 teaspoon salt

Mix all together and freeze.

Serves 6 to 8

Black Cherry Salad

1 jar Bing or black cherries

1 package cherry jello

2 cups hot pineapple juice

1 package cream cheese

½ cup chopped nuts, toasted

Dissolve jello in 2 cups of hot pineapple juice. Stuff Bing cherries with cream cheese and nuts mixed. After jello is cooled arrange in mold with stuffed cherries. Let chill until firm.

Serves 6 to 8

From the left: Grandma Perry, Mom,
Grandmother Tullar, Roni
High School Graduation for Roni

Blue Ribbon Macaroni Salad

4 pounds large elbow macaroni, uncooked
1 (10-ounce) package frozen green peas, cooked and drained
2 cups mayonnaise
1 cup carrots, shredded
¼ cup mixed vegetable flakes
¼ cup parsley flakes
1 tablespoon salt
1 teaspoon black pepper, freshly ground
1 teaspoon onion powder

Cook macaroni according to package directions. Drain well and cool. Stir in remaining ingredients. Chill until ready to serve. Garnish with shredded carrot, if desired.

Serves 48

Corn Bread Salad

6 cups crumbled corn bread
2 cups mayonnaise
2 stalks celery, chopped
1 large green pepper, chopped
2 large tomatoes, diced
¾ cup chopped green onions
¾ cup chopped pecans
1 (4-ounce) jar diced pimento, drained

Combine all ingredients, stirring well. Cover and chill at least 2 hours.

Makes 8 to 10 servings

Corned Beef Salad

1 small package lemon gelatin
1 cup boiling water
1 (12-ounce) can corned beef
1 cup mayonnaise
1 (16-ounce) can green peas, drained
2 cups celery, chopped
1½ tablespoons onion, minced
1½ tablespoons chopped pimento
¼ cup chopped green pepper

Dissolve gelatin in boiling water. Stir in corned beef. Fold in remaining ingredients. Spoon into 8x12-inch dish; chill overnight or until firm. Serve on lettuce leaf.

Serves 12

Crunchy Rotelle Salad

1 cup uncooked rotelle pasta
1 cup frozen English peas, thawed and drained
8 ounces cooked ham, cubed
¼ cup chopped radishes
¼ cup chopped green pepper
¼ cup chopped sweet pickle
¼ cup sweet pickle juice

Combine all ingredients and chill before serving.

Serves 6 to 8

Here's a wonderful picture of Mom and Dad in front of the fireplace in our home in California. This is our home that the earthquake broke in half in 1971. Dad lost his job with John Hancock Insurance and he couldn't find work in the earthquake ravaged economy of LA. Mom and Dad tried to give my sister and her new husband the house, just to take over payments on the $30,000 loan. They wanted a horse instead. The bank repossessed the house.

The economy recovered and two years later the house sold for $125,000. Several years after that the house sold for $250,000. Today it is worth well over half a million dollars—poor Dad— silly sister. Oh well, Dad always says a lesson learned no matter how expensive, is worth its cost, if in the long run it makes you a better person. I sure learned to be careful with investments when building Patti's because of what happened to Mom and Dad back then.

Frozen Fruit Salad

1½ cups mayonnaise
12 ounces cream cheese, softened
2 tablespoons lemon rind, grated
¼ cup powdered sugar
1 (17-ounce) can fruit cocktail, well drained

1 large banana, diced
2 cups fresh strawberries, sliced
2 cups heavy cream, whipped
2 cups fresh or frozen blueberries

Blend mayonnaise and cream cheese. Add lemon rind, sugar, fruit cocktail, banana, strawberries and blueberries. Fold in whipped cream, pour into ice cube trays and freeze.

Cut into squares, serve on lettuce leaves.

Serves 8

Fruit Salad

1 cup diced cantaloupe
1 cup diced fresh peaches

2 packages lemon gelatin
1¾ pints boiling water

Dissolve gelatin in boiling water. Drain fruit and when gelatin is slightly thickened, add fruit.

Serves 8

Glazed Sweet Fruit Salad Dressing

⅓-½ cup sugar
1 teaspoon grated onion
1 teaspoon paprika
1 teaspoon salt

1 teaspoon dry mustard
1 teaspoon celery seed
¼ cup vinegar
1 cup salad oil

Combine sugar, onion, paprika, salt, mustard, celery seed and 1 tablespoon vinegar. Gradually add oil alternately with remaining vinegar. This makes a thick glossy dressing that is wonderful over fresh fruit.

Serves 6

1990 — (from the left) Front row: Grandmother Tullar (Dad's mother) holding Dohnte (Kimberlee's son, Roni's grandson, Patti's great-grandson, Grandmother Tullar's great-great-grandson). Middle row: Mom, Kimberlee (Roni's daughter), Michael Lee, Lawana, Michael Tullar. Back row: Dad, Chip (me)

1999 — (from the left) 1st Row: Anna with Aunt Roni, Arielle with Uncle Chip. 2nd Row: Ashleigh (Craig's daughter), Michael T. with Adam, Lawana, Craig and Michael Lee.

Raspberry Salad

1 (3-ounce) package raspberry
   gelatin
1 cup boiling water

1 (10-ounce) package frozen
   raspberries, drained
1 cup raspberry juice
1 cup applesauce

Combine gelatin and boiling water, mix thoroughly. Add other ingredients, mix. Pour into molds.

Also good with finely chopped celery, toasted pecans and drained crushed pineapple, before congealing.

Serves 6 to 8

Marinated Onion and Tomato Salad

2 large onions
6 large, firm, ripe tomatoes
1 green bell pepper
¾ cup cider vinegar
¼ cup water

1½ teaspoon mustard seed
1½ teaspoon celery seed
½ teaspoon salt
2 tablespoons sugar
1 tablespoon black pepper,
   freshly ground

Peel thinly slice and separate onions into rings. Peel tomatoes and cut into wedges. Cut pepper into thin slices. Place the above in a shallow dish. Combine remaining ingredients in saucepan and bring to a boil, stirring constantly to dissolve sugar. Pour hot mixture over onions, tomatoes and peppers. Chill several hours. A good salad made in advance.

Serves 10 to 12

From the left: Michael Lee, Mom, Chip (me), Dad, Arielle, Michael, Lawana

Stuffed Tomatoes

6 large tomatoes, very ripe
1 cup black-eyed peas, cooked
1 cup baby lima beans, cooked
Salt
⅓ cup olive oil
1 tablespoon fresh parsley, chopped

1 tablespoon balsamic vinegar
2 teaspoons honey
3 tablespoons fresh mint, chopped
Freshly ground black pepper

Slice off the stem end of the tomatoes leaving ⅔ of tomato. Hollow out the tomatoes, reserving all pulp. Salt the tomato "cups" then turn upside down to drain. Coarsely chop all pulp and combine in a large bowl with the remaining ingredients. Fill tomatoes with the bean mixture. Garnish with mint and serve.

Molded Gazpacho

3 envelopes unflavored gelatin
18 ounces tomato juice
⅓ cup red wine vinegar
½ teaspoon salt
Dash of Tabasco
1¼ cups tomatoes, peeled, seeded, and diced
1½ cups cucumbers, pared and diced

½ cup red bell pepper, chopped
4 scallions (white and green parts, finely chopped)
½ cup celery, chopped
1 tablespoon mixed herbs (parsley, tarragon, chives) chopped

Soften the gelatin by sprinkling it over 1 cup tomato juice. Dissolve over low heat, stirring constantly. Remove from heat and blend in remaining tomato juice, vinegar, salt and Tabasco. Refrigerate until mixture is the consistency of unbeaten egg whites (stir occasionally). Fold in tomato, cucumber, red pepper, scallions, celery, and herbs. Pour into a 1½-quart mold that has been rinsed in cold water. Refrigerate 6 hours until firm.

Serves 6 to 8

Mustard Ring

8 eggs, beaten
1½ cups sugar
2 tablespoons dry mustard
1 cup cider vinegar
1 cup water

1 teaspoon salt
2 packages unflavored gelatin
½ cup cold water
1 pint cream, whipped

Mix first six ingredients together in heavy sauce pan. Cook over medium heat, stirring constantly, until custard-like consistency. Dissolve gelatin in water. Stir mixture of gelatin and water into hot custard until dissolved. Remove from heat and cool. When completely cooled fold in whipped cream. Place mixture in mold that has been coated with mayonnaise. When firm, unmold on tray with bed of greens. Garnish with grapes.

Very good with pork!

Serves 8

Chip (me), Gennie Sutherland, Mom and Lawana on a buying trip in the very early years of the gift shop history. Gennie was our next door neighbor in Tucson, Arizona where we children were all born. Gennie's family had four kids, all the same ages as our four. Her son Ron and I were very mischievous. We used to love to play with matches and of course our parents didn't approve. One day we went under their house (to hide from our parents) and started a fire. We nearly burned the place down. Luckily, she loved me and she was like a second mom for most of her life.

At the age of 5, I woke up before everyone else one day, went into the living room and lit a lighter that had been left out. I caught my pajamas on fire and ran into my parents' bedroom crying. My dad jumped up threw me on the floor and rolled me up in a carpet, putting the fire out. My uncle donated blood which was used to help save my life. I still have several scars to remind me of my foolish ways that evidently started very early in my life. Hopefully, I'm a little wiser now.

Texas Caviar Salad

2 (15-ounce) cans black-eyed
   peas, drained
½ cup chopped purple onion
½ cup chopped green pepper
½ clove garlic

¼ cup vinegar
¼ cup vegetable oil
¼ cup sugar
⅛ teaspoon salt
⅛ teaspoon pepper

Combine first 4 ingredients in a large bowl. Combine remaining ingredients in a jar; cover and shake well. Pour over vegetables; toss lightly. Cover and chill 12 hours. Remove garlic and drain before serving.

Serves 6 to 8

Tomato Aspic with Artichoke

3 ounces lemon gelatin
1 teaspoon Knox gelatin
1¾ cups hot & spicy V-8 juice
¼ cup white vinegar

½ teaspoon salt
¼ teaspoon ground cloves
1 can drained artichoke hearts –
   not marinated

Dissolve gelatin in tomato juice, add vinegar, salt and cloves. Chill until consistency of egg whites. Place one artichoke in individual molds that have been lightly coated with mayonnaise or cooking spray. Pour gelatin over artichoke hearts and refrigerate until firm.

Serves 6 to 8

Introducing my mother, the warm, sophisticated, graceful, talented, and gorgeous model at Patti's on the Pier. Mom loved bright colors. I seem to have inherited that same trait. Being colorful is one of my strongest characteristics too. Then, look at what Dad wears; bright blue, yellow and red Heehaw overalls. What would you expect of me?

Summer Tomato Pasta Salad

1 (6-ounce) package spiral or shell
   pasta
6 fresh tomatoes, peeled and
   chopped
½ onion, chopped
2 stalks celery, chopped

½ green pepper, chopped
3 tablespoons vegetable or olive
   oil
7 tablespoons red wine vinegar
1 tablespoon sugar
Salt and freshly ground pepper, to
   taste

Cook pasta according to package directions using minimum cooking time.
Drain and rinse with cold water. Drain well! Combine with remaining ingredients; toss lightly. Chill several hours before serving

Makes 8 cups

Tossed Crab Louis Salad

6 ounces frozen or canned
   crabmeat
½ cup sliced cauliflower
½ cup sliced celery
½ cup sliced green pepper
1 tomato, cut in wedges

½ cup cucumber chunks
½ cup Thousand Island dressing
1 teaspoon lemon juice
4 lettuce leaves
2 cups shredded lettuce
2 hard-boiled eggs, quartered

Thaw crab, if necessary. Reserve 4 pieces of crab for garnish. Drain and
flake remaining crab. Combine crab, cauliflower, celery, green pepper,
cucumber, dressing and lemon juice on each of 4 lettuce lined plates, place
½ cup shredded lettuce and ¼ cup crab mixture. Garnish with whole crab
pieces, tomato and eggs.

Makes 4 servings

Here's Mother in Hee Haw overalls, just like Dad's. She's talking with Katherine Sanders, our first landscape manager, about landscape development, the overalls—or whatever. Mom and Dad both always have a dog or two (or a miniature pig) in tow.

Michael Lee and Grandmother Tullar reading the sensual *"Playboar"* magazine—Calvin Swine really loved the centerfold.

Here, Mom and I are on vacation in Cancun. We're both dressed in blue and white. It happened frequently, we were so much alike, that we'd walk out of our respective rooms and find ourselves in the same type or same colored outfits.

Here, Mom and I are in Jamaica, our last trip. Look how much alike we are dressed. I think we just loved each other so much there must have been some sort of telepathy going on.

"Welcome to my house" Mom always opened her house to everyone. Dad's the same way — they never met a stranger.

Here, Mom sits in Dad's chair holding Arielle (Mike and Lawana's first child). Notice that Mom is always smiling. There was so much love in her personality, which luckily is a Tullar family trait.

Here, Mom is being serenaded by Mike Flatt and his partner Charlie Baker. Mike's parents were Mom and Dad's very first customers at the old Grand Rivers Motel. Mike and I became very best friends over the years and he was the first person in my life to call me his best friend.

It seems I always fell short for some reason with others, but Mike was going through a time in life where I guess my friendship was pretty important. Twenty-four years later we're still best friends and Mike and Charlie and Michael Lee and I have taken more than 10 trips together. Mother was often an honored guest on these trips. Here we are on our last trip to Jamaica (where we wrote our first cookbook, it's necessary to get away in order to be able to concentrate on these things). Believe it or not, Mike actually has a spectacular voice, and Mom enjoyed this rendition.

Mike has been suffering from a life threatening illness for the past couple of years and told me how he was afraid of dying. This feeling was especially intense when going to sleep because the doctors were afraid of heart failure while sleeping because he has sleep apnea. He explains to me today he's not afraid of dying any more and has given me this thought to contemplate.

"The memories we create today become our dreams for tomorrow."

He goes on to say that now, when he goes to sleep, he dreams a lot. He dreams about things that happened yesterday; things like going to the ice cream parlor with his grandfather, fishing with his dad when he was a little boy, walking down the road to his aunt and uncle's farm, building sand castles at the beach when he was little. Now he goes to sleep and he's not afraid of dying. He's excited about a possible walk through the night with his memories of life, good for you, Mike.

Folks, most people say you walk through life and can count your friends on one hand. I've been so lucky. I'd need my fingers and toes. I've come to the conclusion that what you get out of life is in a direct proportion to what you put into it. Take Jesus as an example. He walked around spreading love, teaching us not to judge one another but to love one another. Just think how much he was loved in return. Wouldn't it be nice if the politicians and church leaders of today stopped legislating morality but rather, promoted the idea that we should love one another. We could more easily turn the other cheek when someone tries to harm us instead of struggling with vengeance all the time. Mike, I love you as a best friend after all these years because you're so much like me. You love to make life easier for everyone around you. You love to make people laugh even at your own expense and you love to entertain. Thanks, my friend, for being a friend and thanks for allowing yours and Charlie's house to be a place where I could wake up every morning and write this book uninterrupted. One more memory in a walk together.

Arielle, this picture is for you — you were your grandmother's first grandchild to live close by. She adored you, and here you and she are sharing a story of some kind. Storytelling is another Tullar trait and I think you've inherited that trait too!

Mom and Irene (who owns the Lite Side Café in Grand Rivers) on a trip to Mexico. Irene started by selling us the homemade candies for our gift shop and was so successful she opened her own business down the street from Patti's. We became even closer friends and Irene went to Mexico with us and 4 other lady friends of Mother's. I had 6 women to keep track of for 7 days. Boy, I was deserving of a medal for that trip.

Mom, with one of her best friends in the world, Anne Ireland. Anne and Jack, her husband, own The Silvercliff Inn in old Kuttawa. Jack, Dad and I all worked for the Small Business Administration's Disaster Office. Jack was one of our bosses. He worked in the area and fell in love with the lakes region. He and Anne retired here and now they run one of the finest guest houses in the country. They are positively charming hosts. Phone # (270) 388-5858 e-mail: www.kentuckylake.com/silvercliff

We spent 2 days in Helen, GA on our trip to FL with Marion. Here are some more shots of that trip.

From the left: Me, Mom and Michael Lee in the quaint alpine village in North Georgia, Helen.

From the left: Patti, Michael Lee and Marion. As you can see, Mom really loved Michael Lee—just as she did everyone—she was a neat lady.

Marion (who has been with us at Patti's longer than anyone else) and Mom in Helen, GA. We're on our trip to Florida to retrieve Marion's memories from her vacation home there after her husband Frank (our Santa Claus when we entertained the handicapped children at Christmas) passed away.

From the left: Marion, Ellen, Mom, Gennie, Lawana, me. We're at market in Atlanta, all smiles even after a long, hard day. Who doesn't like to shop?

Mom with the catch of the day— look at that smile.

Now, here's Dad, the patriarch of the family, and as it was when we were growing up, always taking pictures. Here, he and Mom are celebrating their 50th wedding anniversary at the Irelands' Silver Cliff Inn Bed and Breakfast.

Here, Dad has one of his fine feathered friends, Mother Goose. He's entertaining our guests, young and old.

Here's a great picture of Dad and his handyman son, Craig—notice the animals—Mom's German shepherd, Tyla, and my dog from Hawaii, Pow, while Craig holds a box turtle from the yard. Craig's the least animal loving of us children. Notice his expression, "YUCK". Craig was the fix-it-all man of the family while we were growing up. Craig and Dad loved tinkering with things together. I was the student who couldn't fix anything. Michael watched hours of TV. Roni ran with her friends.

This picture was most likely taken on Sunday after church. Sunday was our family day—church first, then yard work for all three boys, house cleaning for the girls and grilling out in the evening. It was one of our best days as a family. Then, we kids grew older and our circle of friends began to pull us away from our family unit. But we did always have a beautiful yard with a smashing rose garden.

Dad, like so many in the country, fell in love with miniature pigs. He became famous with his miniature pigs. Here we have him with Belle—as in "Belle of the Lakes." She went to the house every day and night with Dad and slept in the same room with him. Four dogs, two cats and Belle the pig shared their bungalow.

Dad once told me, "Son, it doesn't matter to what length you go to get free publicity, just get your name out there." Remember, this is the same man who came home with 12 baby ducks on a post Easter day just because they were on sale. He took them to Patti's on the Pier which was located at one of the two resort marinas in town, Green Turtle Bay.

The first year they were cute and unique and everyone loved them. Then they took to sitting and messing on the boaters' swim platforms during the winter months to get out of the cold water. This was OK because no one was home on the boats. Spring came and the duck population grew. The boat owners returned and became more and more upset because of the messes on their swim platforms. The coups-de-gras came when the ducks kept everyone awake with their quacking. All they wanted was to be fed. Soon, there was a boater led recall of the ducks.

Well, how did Dad handle this revolt? He called Channel 6 TV and Sam Burrage, always looking for a good human-interest story, came out and filmed "the great Green Turtle Bay duck round-up." We made the 6 o'clock and 10 o'clock news casts with that one—go, Dad, go.

Dad and Calvin Swine, the lemonade drinking pig.

Calvin was Dad's first pig and he grew to weigh several hundred pounds. Subsequently, Calvin became the first Patti's Animal Park animal. He became so popular because he loved to drink cola drinks (the sugary type, no diet for this pig) out of a fruit jar. He'd stand up on his hind legs and drink and quickly became the most photographed entity at Patti's. He was on the television show *Tennessee Crossroads,* on the news in Evansville and in several newspapers. He became so popular that Dad installed a phone on the side of his house for the kids to call Calvin at home. Dad's greatest promotional dream was to have the *USA Today* newspaper brought to him from Deweese's IGA and find himself with Calvin on the front page. Unfortunately, it still hasn't happened but maybe someday the grandchildren will pick up on their grandfather's past and make this dream come true.

Dad's success with Calvin led to the development of old Mr. Bill's farm—now called Miss Mary's Petting Farm. He had all kinds of animals, especially babies that he'd rotate out with local farmers. This way he always had a crop of new baby animals as larger animals tend to scare our younger guests.

This is Dad today. He doesn't get out much anymore unless the weather's nice, but he still wears his Heehaw overalls every day. They are his uniform and since he never knows when a Patti's friend may stop by he's always dressed and ready to be Mr. Bill. Dad and I play double solitaire every day now and where some may think of it as a waste of time, I look at it as getting Dad (and all his wisdom, advice and stories) all to myself. His stories are still wonderful. We made a great team playing cards when I was younger and I guess we always will be.

My dad is such a remarkable man. He not only gave me his name as his oldest son, but he gave me his looks too.

He's always such an optimist—always trying to make himself and his relationship with life a greater success. I'd like to take a moment and tell you some fond memories I have with Dad. One I'll cherish most is when he came home with his reel to reel tape deck—oh, the music was so beautiful sounding and lasted 2 hours on each reel. His and Mom's favorites were the big band music and Mom had it playing all afternoon when we'd come home from school—remember we still didn't have TV yet. I developed the greatest appreciation for music because of that reel to reel tape player. That appreciation might help to explain why I started two successful dance clubs in Paducah. Then there was the 8 mm movie camera Dad used to take movies of my 4th birthday party. There, with a duck in our small backyard pool, was my mother's father, my Grandfather Perry, who I would have no recollection of at all if not for that camera. I remember him waving to the camera—and me and my new duck—what a picture! And my dad had captured it on film for me.

I love my dad so much. He was and still is a great mentor for me. When I was eight he brought home a cribbage set and taught me how to play cribbage. It was so smart of him. Years later he tells me I was having trouble with math in school and the counselors had told him to play games with me (fifteen two fifteen four and pair is six and pair is eight). I eventually became a math and science major in high school. There are so many fond memories of my dad and throughout this book I hope to share more since I shared so many of Mom's in the first cookbook.

When I was 10, my parents started teaching me how to play bridge, the card game. On weekends, they would get together with friends and play bridge by the hours—laughing, yelling, making jokes—they had the best time and I could stay up later if I kept quiet and was the gopher boy—you know, go for this and go for that. Anyway, Dad would let me watch and eventually I learned how to play. So Dad and I would play against Mom and Grandmother (Mom's mother who lived with us). Dad and I almost always won. We were truly a great team and still are. You know, back in those days Dad worked six days a week, 10 to 12 hours a day. The few minutes and hours we had together were lots of fun. I wish there had been more but I treasure the ones we had and especially the ones we have now. I love you, Dad.

Dad always was politically minded. From president of the PTA and homeowner's association to the Grand Rivers city council—a duty he still enjoys. Pictured from the left: Dale Totten, Dad, Livingston County Judge Executive Ralph Smith, Mayor Frank Buchanon, former Mayor (for over 25 years) and present council member John Henry O'Bryan, Jeff Deweese who owns the local IGA grocery store, John Henry's grandson Randy O'Bryan, and John Henry's daughter Betty Stiles. All but Mr. Smith and Mr. Buchanan are council members. Remember, ours is a very small town so it should come as no surprise that one family has three members on the council.

Here I am—stepping out a little. It seems for years I just stood in the background. With the passing of Mom and with Dad's retirement, I took over the visible reins of Patti's just for a short while. My brother, his wife and their lovely family really make better family role models and today have taken over the role as the out front family in our family business.

I'll take just a brief moment to say a little about myself. I really feel that I've been a major influence in the development of Patti's to date. The inspiration for that influence has come from people who dream and live life to the fullest while pursuing their dream in this great country of ours; Walt Disney (Disneyland), Ray Kroc (McDonald's), Sam Walton (Walmart) and Ronald Reagan to name just a few.

Mr. Disney, with his development of the world's greatest family entertainment center, is truly my inspiration and my hero.

I'm pictured here with one of my most prized possessions, a Christmas gift from my managers. It is a statue of Mickey Mouse painting Walt Disney who he sees while looking in a mirror at himself. It illustrates that the creation is really an extension of the man. I just hope you can feel my influence when you walk around Patti's today.

Here I am at the proudest point in my early life. This is my commissioning picture in 1971, Ensign William Grant Tullar, Jr. Notice the handlebar mustache. It was the talk of the base. People could recognize me from the rear just by the mustache. I went to Explosive Ordinance Disposal school in Indian Head, Maryland for a year of training and then on to Fort Story, Virginia.

I was running 5 miles a day and swimming a mile twice a week. I had a Nuclear Weapons Design Information Clearance, one of the highest security clearances in the country. I was truly very proud of who I was and what I had accomplished at age 23. My parents were proud of me too, which was one of the reasons I had worked so hard.

I, being a Jr. and the oldest son, always looked at Dad as a role model and tried to emulate him. Like him, I try to be the leader of any group to which I belong. It started when I became freshman class president in college.

In the top photo, here I am as president of the Kentucky Restaurant Association. We're discussing the endorsement of then candidate Paul Patton, who I recognized early on to be an outstanding candidate for governor. I supported him before the Kentucky Restaurant Association's Board of Directors endorsed him for governor.

I really enjoyed my four years as an officer of the association and it was a tremendous learning experience. I am still on the Board of Directors as a past president.

Pictured here in 1999, Roni, Sophie (my younger daughter in the rhinestone collar), and me. My sister, Roni, and I are very close now and have been for years. She's such a wonderful person, it would be hard for anyone not to love her. As we've gotten older it's amazing how much she looks like Mom and I look like Dad, and Sophie looks like her dad (me).

This is Michael Lee, Patti's Guy Friday, who does just about everything with his oldest daughter, Sadie. He is a past member of the city council, past president of the Chamber of Commerce, head of Grand Rivers' beautification committee and a member of the Livingston County Literacy Council.

He's everyone's friend because he's always ready, willing and able to help someone else even before being asked. A graduate of Murray State University, Michael is loved by everyone he meets.

Here's one of my personal favorite pictures. As you can see, he's cute as a button. At 45, he hates being called cute. He always says, "how old do I have to be before people stop calling me cute?" I tell him, "the time's coming but 'till then, lucky you."

Pictured here is Hazel Demery, one of the grand matriarchs of Grand Rivers and head of the Livingston County Democratic party. The party hasn't lost an election in our county since she's been in charge. She and Mike endlessly lobby for assistance in the development of our community. Mike wrote letters and Hazel lobbied in person for lighting on I-24 at our Grand Rivers exit. They go in this year, 2000.

Here are Lawana and Michael Lee hard at work sawing logs after a day of touring Gatlinburg to see what we could learn to make our town better. The night before, we were all up late watching the news. Our government had just started bombing Iraq in an attempt to contain Sadam Hussein. Mike

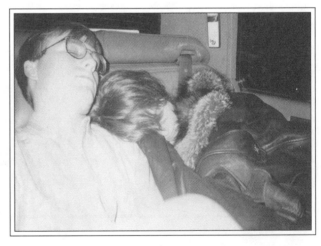

and Lawana are best buddies and their jobs often overlap—with the exception of raising children. Michael Lee's two daughters, Sadie and Sophie, each have four legs and a tail. Lawana's are the traditional type, two girls and a boy (two legs, no tails).

Michael Lee, Sadie, Sophie and me on the front porch of our house which looks over Patti's Settlement. Originally Thomas Lawson's house (the man that founded Grand Rivers in 1890), it is listed in the National Register of Historic Places and is a Kentucky Landmark.

An unknown mummy, Mike Nance as the Incredible Hulk, Michael T. as an Indian guru, Lawana as a belly dancer and a friend, all get into the spirit of Halloween.

Here's Michael Tullar at his eighth birthday party (count the candles) with his cat Popoké (a Hawaiian name). Michael T. is still a cat lover. Can't you see how important animals are to our family. It breaks my heart when someone thinks our family is cruel to animals. One time a customer called the humane society and reported us for cruelty to animals. She had gone out to the llama and burro pen and seen two empty plastic buckets hanging on the fence so she reported us for lack of attention to our animals (no water). The game officers came out, told us they were there to investigate this complaint, and we walked out in disbelief to see what the problem could be. To no one's surprise, we discovered the empty feed buckets. After being fed, the buckets were always empty within 30 minutes. They weren't water buckets to begin with. There was plenty of water on hand in a separate area of the pen. The game wardens just shook their heads and went on. Oh well.

Now, we have Michael T. as a husband, father and as overseer of the building of Patti's. He's the former head of Patti's on the Pier, former kitchen manager of Patti's and now President of Patti's Enterprises, LLC. He's father to Arielle, Anna and Adam. Mike's pictured here with his and Lawana's first child, Arielle, who has a miniature golf course named after her.

Arielle, Anna and Adam are lucky children indeed. The live in a household where their parents love each other very much. But then, their parents, Michael and Lawana were lucky enough to grow up in loving homes. Both the Tullar and the Greenlee homes were wonderful role models for raising families.

This is probably one of my favorite pictures of my brother. He is so gifted when it comes to building and really enjoys it. He was in charge of taking down the log cabin which became Ashleigh's Boutique and moving it to the settlement and rebuilding it. During this rebuilding, a huge beam fell and struck him on the back of the neck, coming within a fraction of an inch of killing or paralyzing him. Seeing him in this picture working makes me thankful God left him here to continue being the major part of Patti's that he is, but more importantly, to be a father for his children.

Michael T. and I are brothers and partners in the ownership of Patti's. Here we are in Washington, DC at the Small business Administration's reception for all 50 state winners of the small business of the year. We won the state honors in 1995. Michael and I (along with the other winners) were supposed to meet the President. Michael is a staunch Republican who couldn't have cared less about meeting President Clinton. But for me, it was a lifelong goal to meet a President. I would love to have met President Reagan, but it didn't happen. I respected the fact that this man was our president. Well, it turned out that Mr. Clinton wasn't going to meet with all of us and would be the first President in the program's history not to meet with the winners. Well, I was so disappointed at missing this life-long dream fulfillment of mine that I started complaining. With the help of the woman who won from Georgia, we complained and complained and complained—but to no avail.

Then, my brother got interviewed on CNN about the situation and he really hit a nerve. The next day, our last day there, we were whisked off to the White House executive office building. Out came the President. I was thrilled. I went up to shake his hand after his talk, but Mike stood back beholden to his principles. Then he weakened and came forward and ended up getting his hand shaken by the President not once, but twice. And to all his Republican friends, I saw Michael Tullar do it with a smile on his face. With this writing, it will go down in history. He really was a good sport after all. I'll bet you today that he denies it to his Republican friends.

The kicker happened the next morning. I was checking out of the hotel at 11:30 and at that time was given a message that had come in the prior evening. The president's secretary had called and invited my family and me to a private meeting and breakfast at the White House at 7:30 that morning. We didn't get the message until 11:30 that morning. I was so angry that to this day I detest that hotel for their incompetence. Oh well, maybe I'll have another opportunity. I'll always work toward that goal anyway.

Christmas, 1998, at my house. Lawana holding Adam, Michael holding Anna and the lovely Miss Arielle kneeling.

January 2000—from the left: Anna, Lawana, Arielle, Michael and Adam—the next generation of Tullars. May theirs be as fun and fulfilling a life, blessed with heartwarming memories and great people, as mine has been.

Arielle, Anna and Adam already hard at work marketing the bears in the Wagon Wheel for the new brochure pictures. When you see them be sure to say "hi". Arielle, remember, is quite a story teller. Anna likes to build like her grandpa Norvell (Patti's chief carpenter) and Adam, well, he's still just enjoying being the baby. Oh Lordy, he'll probably follow in his father's footsteps. Michael was the baby as well and he sure was spoiled as the youngest of the four of us.

The future challenges all of us to greatness. Pictured below, some of the movers and shakers—watch us grow.

Top: Grandpa Norvell Greenlee and Adam, 1999. Center (from the left): Anna, Michael T., Adam, Arielle. Top row: Grandma Rose and Grandpa Norvell. Sitting: Michael T. holding Adam and Arielle, Lawana holding Anna. Bottom (in the pool, from the left): Arielle, Anna, Lawana, Adam

The pictures included here are Adam on his new tractor with Grandpa Norvell giving his first driving lesson. Adam is the first and probably only Tullar grandson. He will have many challenges in life in carrying on the family name. I know, to some degree, having the honor of carrying my dad's name. I'm William Grant Tullar, Jr., alias "Chip", because Dad already used the name Bill. Since I looked like a chipmunk with a mouth full of nuts (Adam has those same full cheeks), I was nicknamed Chip. Hence, my lifelong name. Adam will be assisted in life by the watchful eyes of his grandfather who is truly one of the most creative craftsmen anywhere around. I'm sure tractoring will be only one of many lessons his grandfather will give him.

Arielle, Anna and Adam absolutely adore their father, Michael. You can bet he's a very proud papa, too. When Mike comes home from work, the children clamor for his attention. Michael is living a life that very closely parallels the life he experienced growing up. While growing up the baby, maybe he was able to absorb more of our family's lessons on successful parenting. I wish him and his family as much love and success as we children had with our parents. I can only hope if each of us learns from our parents, both the successful and not so successful traits of parenting, then each generation will be a little wiser than the last. May there always be as much love in this family as there is now.

Lawana, daughter of Norvell and Rose is pictured here teaching the kids how to swim. Folks, Lawana is a jewel you don't get to run into very often. Lawana worked her way through college while being a hostess at Patti's on the Pier. She and Mike were married in 1991 and soon started their family. Lawana and I became senior host and hostess at Patti's. After the birth of Adam, she has greatly reduced her work as Patti's hostess. She now is a full time mom and works with Mike at home on computer graphics for the Settlement. She makes sure the children's lives are filled with activities such as ballet, piano, gymnastics, singing, cheerleading and church. It's a full time schedule for any mom. Most importantly, Lawana makes sure the children are right with their understanding of our Lord. I'm very proud of her as a sister-in-law, mom, wife, friend and since Mom's passing, the matriarch of the Tullar family as it grows into the 21st century. Good luck. You're a great one, one I'm sure has Mom smiling with joy in Heaven.

Folks, these are the next generations of our family along with all the employees. Kids like Justin and Jonathan, Zach and Ryan, Mauri and Matthew, Lincoln, Jansen and Casey just to name a few. As you can see, I will have plenty of stories for the next book.

This is a photo taken at one of our Christmas parties which until 1999, we always held as a pot luck at Mr. Bill's restaurant. Here, Arielle is maybe 2 years old, so it must have been about 1995. On Arielle's left, you see Lawana's parents, the ever picture shy Grandma Rose and the ever handy Grandpa Norvell.

1999 was our second year without Mom. Front row: Ashleigh (Craig's daughter, the namesake for Ashleigh's Boutique); Anna (Anna's Emporium); Arielle (Arielle's Miniature Golf). Second row: my sister, Roni; Dad; Lawana with Adam. Back row: Michael Lee holding Sadie; me holding Sophie; Craig; Michael T. (the Lee and T. after both Michaels is to help keep confusion to a minimum).

Entreés, Breads, Casseroles,
Brunch & Beverages

The Patti's Family - Growing
1977

with development of
Hamburger Patti's Ice Cream Parlor

I'm Happy Being Me

Imagine how happy
            And free I could be
If I took me a little less seriously—
    If I'd laugh at my faults
            Every once in a while,
And accept my mistakes
            With a shrug and a smile,
If I'd take little setbacks
            And failures in stride,
    And remember successes
            With pleasure and pride—

    Imagine how happy
            And free I could be
If I did all I could
            To enjoy being me!

Handmade quilts, an abundance of flowers, great food, a warm home, Mom's influence everywhere, even homemade apple pie—it's all here at Patti's 1880's Settlement.

Pictured above, you see Curtis and Norma playfully enjoying each other's company and the good food their name is synonymous with.

"We have worked on an exciting book, creating a cookbook you'll have to have even if you don't like to cook—cooking made easy."
Curtis and Norma Grace

I'd like to give special thanks to two of my dearest friends, Curtis and Norma Grace. Curtis and Norma helped in the development and presentation of the recipes in this book, hence, the "Grace" of *"The Grace of Patti's."* Curtis, Mom and I became friends after attending an auction of the "House of Grace" in May 1977. Mom and I were looking for a fat fryer and met Curtis. He invited us to come see his 9th Street House Restaurant.

The House of Grace was moving to a new location and into a 19th Century Queen Anne Victorian home similar in architecture to our own Thomas Lawson/Tullar home. Situated on 9th Street in Paducah, it was called "The Ninth Street House." Curtis was owner/chef of this fabulous restaurant until its closing in 1998, when he joined our staff as chief culinary consultant. Curtis studied under renowned chefs like Julie Dannenbaum, Julia Childs and James Beard. Curtis is the author of four cookbooks of his own: *Cooking with Curtis Grace; Cook Talk with Curtis Grace and Friends; A Little Touch of Grace;* and *Encore*.

Curtis and Norma have been married for 47 years. They have four sons; Curtis Allen, Jay, Tim and Brian. These boys have given them seven grandchildren and three great-grandchildren.

After meeting Curtis, Mom and I developed our friendship with him which would last our lifetimes. In our first year, we were hardly ever busy, so I'd go cook at the Ninth Street House on Saturday nights. I learned so much from Curtis including the basics that led to the development of our famous pork chop seasoning. Today, Curtis and Norma and I are working on an extremely special tea recipe which we hope to market with our newest joint effort, *The Grace of Patti's*. May each and every one of you enjoy the love Curtis and I have for each other in bringing these wonderful, easy to cook, delicious, country American recipes from our hearts to you.

Anna's Cheesy Tortilla

Soft taco size, flour tortillas
Sliced individually wrapped
American cheese

Sour cream

Spread 1 teaspoon of sour cream on a flour tortilla then top with a slice of cheese. Roll tortilla up and place in microwave for 20 seconds.

To add interest: ½ teaspoon of your favorite salsa on the cheese before placing in the microwave.

"Be careful the cheese will be hot! I like these for lunch. My Aunt Roni told me how to fix these. I can fix these myself."

Contributed by Anna Tullar, February 2000, age 4 years

In the Beginning

Most of you know Mom (Miss Patti) and Dad (Mr. Bill). This photo was probably one of their best pictures. It was taken in 1971 while we were on a weekend vacation while I was at Officers' Candidate School in Newport, RI. We're in Vermont in a setting not unlike Patti's today. As I grew up I never saw or heard my parents fight. I was 18 when I left for college and I can remember that I always wanted to have a marriage just like theirs.

They loved each other so much. It seemed like my friends, for the most part, didn't have as happy a home life as I had and were always coming over to play because Mom always had fresh baked goods waiting for us kids and our friends. I learned years later that they did fuss with one another—but it was always behind closed doors.

Thanks Mom and Dad for that consideration. You'll never know how much that meant to me. Mom and Dad were together 54 years when the Lord called Mom to his arms. Dad's now 78 and very lonely without her, although he still has a few good friends, his miniature pinchers Elkie and Sassy, his family and his still vivid memories. They were so beautifully happy together and you can still see that when you walk in the house.

Dad came to Grand Rivers in 1975 and stayed in the Newcomb's Modern Cabins motel and fell in love with the area. To make a long story short, he bought the motel for $19,000 and moved Mom and Grandma to Kentucky from Florida. He was always gone on the road working for the SBA's disaster office (FEMA handles this today) and in 1977 Mom got the idea to open a hamburger and ice cream parlor. I laughed when she asked Michael Lee and me to come to Kentucky from Los Angeles and go into business with her. I turned her down. Then Dad got on the phone and offered us half the business after 5 years if we'd move back and go into business with him. I just chuckled—here I was in graduate school, getting my master's degree in marriage and family counseling and Michael Lee was taking pre-veterinary classes—and they wanted us to come flip hamburgers for a living. Well, I was voted 19 out of 20 to be the least sought after therapist in my therapy studies course because I couldn't keep a secret (I always talked about what my then client and I were discussing—I thought it was part of the class). Also, we were robbed 5 times in a year since we were poor college students living in a poor section of the city! Then there was the smog and the traffic. So, we packed our bags and moved from a city of millions to a hamlet of 350 residents (Grand Rivers) in March of 1977 to open Hamburger Patti's Ice Cream Parlor. Cute name, huh? How could I resist Mom and Dad's calls for help with a name like that to come home to?

Dad got to come home every couple of months between disasters and we were really struggling. If he, Michael Lee and I hadn't worked other jobs, Patti's would never have survived its first five years. One day a dear friend, Pat Moore, painted an old milk can with roses and Patti's logo and gave it to Dad. When he was home from his government job, he would tend to our rose gardens. He'd go out to the gardens, cut fresh roses, then take them to all the local hotels, motels and resorts. He'd put his fresh roses in a bud vase next to our brochures at each lodging facility and get to know all the staff members and before you know it, people started coming to eat with us. After a while, we started to grow. After a few years, Dad came home for good.

Arielle's Crispy Baked Chicken

½ cup cornmeal
½ cup all-purpose flour
½ teaspoon salt
1½ teaspoon chili powder
½ teaspoon dried oregano

¼ teaspoon pepper
3½ pound chicken or chicken strips
⅓ cup butter or margarine
Patti's Barbeque Sauce

Combine first six ingredients. Dip chicken in milk, then roll in cornmeal mixture. Place in greased 13x9-inch pan. Drizzle with butter. Bake uncovered at 375° for 55 minutes. If using strips cooking time will be approximately 25 to 30 minutes.

Serves 10 to 12

"This is my favorite way to eat chicken. My Grandma Rose first fixed it for me — now Mom fixes it too. My favorite is chicken strips. I like to dip my chicken in our barbeque sauce."

Contributed by Arielle Tullar, February 2000, age 7 years.

Baked Chili Spaghetti

1 package spaghetti
¾ pound ground round steak
2 tablespoons chili powder (mix into meat)
2 medium onions, chopped
1 green pepper, chopped
Bacon drippings
1 can tomatoes
1 medium can mushrooms, chopped

1 tablespoon Worcestershire sauce
8 shakes hot sauce
3 tablespoons chili powder (mix in sauce)
Salt and pepper
½ pound sharp cheese, grated
Catsup
½ cup buttered bread crumbs

Cook spaghetti in boiling water for 20 minutes, or until tender. Brown onion, pepper and seasoned meat in bacon drippings. Mix with tomatoes, mushrooms, Worcestershire sauce, hot sauce, chili, salt, pepper and most of the cheese. Add cooked spaghetti, mix well. Place in buttered baking dish, top with rest of cheese, catsup and crumbs. Bake in oven at 350° for 30 to 45 minutes. Can be mixed beforehand and kept in refrigerator.

Serves 8

Here's Mom in 1977, back in the kitchen, then a total space of 8' × 15'. It is now part of our dining room we call the Crown Room. If you look at the stained glass window in the rear of the room, it is about where the window is in this photo. Our first uniforms were red and white checkered shirts with bib overalls. We had one Jenn-Aire stove and that was it!

The original kitchen was 450 sq. ft. in size. Today, we have over 3500 sq. ft. of space in our kitchen. We had one stove then, now we have 12 stoves and ovens. Originally we had a 3-hole sink for washing pots and pans only, we served on paper. Today, our dishwashers (anywhere from 2 to 10 people in that department on a shift) wash the dishes and pots and pans for up to 1300 people on a busy Saturday night, 2000 people all day. Our current dishwasher is 24 feet long. We had only a home-style refrigerator to begin with, now we have 4 huge walk-in refrigerators and freezers along with 11 reach-in refrigerators, some huge, some smaller. We have a bakery. We have 2 large cooking lines, each with a large charbroiler, sauté station, fry station and plate running area. We have a prep station. We have 2 dry storage areas. We have 2 large salad & dessert stations. We might have up to 20 cooks on a busy shift whereas in the beginning we couldn't even keep 1 cook busy. It's not the same place it used to be.

How do you like Mom's middle 70's Afro haircut? We never stopped kidding Mom about her new country look.

Baked Stuffed Spareribs

2½ cups coarse bread crumbs
1 egg, beaten
½ cup chopped celery
¼ cup diced onion
1 tablespoon sage

1 teaspoon salt
½ teaspoon pepper
2 medium-size slabs pork
   spareribs
1 (16-ounce) can sauerkraut

Preheat the oven to 325°. Combine the bread crumbs, egg, celery, onion, sage, salt and pepper in a bowl and mix well. Layer the ribs, stuffing mixture and sauerkraut ½ at a time in a medium-size roasting pan. Bake, covered, for 1 to 1½ hours or until ribs are tender and cooked through. (Try baking potatoes in with the ribs). Good!

Serves 4

Barbecued Rabbit

1 rabbit, cut in pieces
1 stick margarine
Salt and pepper to taste
¼ cup vinegar
¼ cup Worcestershire sauce

1 tablespoon sugar
Juice of 1 lemon
Dash Tabasco sauce
1 cup tomato catsup

Cook rabbit slowly in margarine until blood is cooked out (about 30 minutes). Salt and pepper generously. Mix other ingredients and pour over rabbit. Simmer until meat falls from bone, about 2 hours.

Doves and squirrel may be cooked this same way.

Serves 4 to 6

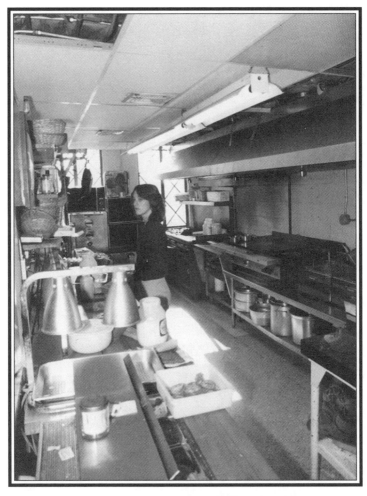

This is how our kitchen looked in roughly 1983 or 1984 after several remodelings. Presently, this area is part of the Crown Room and our wait station at Patti's. The space holding the window and frying pans in the previous picture has been filled in with stoves and hoods in this picture.

Beef & Bean Burritos

1   **pound ground beef**

Brown and drain the beef, prepare with a package of taco or burrito seasoning following package instructions.

2   **(15-ounce) cans pinto beans, mashed**
1   **(10-ounce) can tomatoes and chiles, drained and diced**
1   **(2.25-ounce) can black olives, drained and sliced**
1   **(8-ounce) bag of shredded cheddar cheese**

8   **burrito size flour tortillas**
Sour cream
Guacamole
Shredded lettuce
Diced tomatoes

Preheat oven to 350°. Combine first 3 ingredients and ½ of the can of black olives and warm on stovetop. Spoon mixture into a burrito (DO NOT OVERSTUFF). Fold ends then roll up. Continue process with all 8 tortillas. Spray glass baking dish with nonstick spray. Place burritos next to each other with edges touching — do not stack. Cover with cheddar cheese and place in oven for 10 minutes or until cheese is melted. Serve with sour cream, guacamole, shredded lettuce, diced tomatoes, and the rest of the black olives.

Instead of ground beef, you may use chicken or use black beans. For veggie burritos, use shredded zucchini and yellow squash instead of ground beef. Use mozzarella cheese for topping. These can be frozen and reheated in the microwave.

This recipe submitted by Lawana Tullar.

Serves 4 to 6

If I may, I'd like to talk about Grandmother Tullar (Dad's mom) just a little. A tough old German girl, if I ever saw one—she's about 94 in this photo, blind, hard of hearing, confined to a wheelchair—yet she knew every price of every item in her store by memory (you only had to tell her once). She had all her money down pat by size and would play dumb and ask you what size bill you gave her to make change. Her old buddy, Sam Burrage from WPSD-TV 6 did a story on her back in the middle 80's. She was remarkable. She worked up until the last 3 weeks of her life. When given a 10% chance of survival with an operation and sure death in 24 hours without it, she took her 10% chance and had the surgery. But, she lost her fight with death a few hours later. She loved life so much. She had a spirit that has passed down throughout our entire family. Here, you see her with her old buddy, Jim Farrell.

Because of Grandmother, we are here today and can tell our story. You see, I had gone off to college. A few years later, Dad lost his job when he was 50 years old. There were no age discrimination laws then and it seemed that few were willing to hire someone that age. The Northridge earthquake of 1971 caused extensive damage to our Granada Hills home. Between the loss of income and the earthquake, Dad and Mom lost virtually everything. Dad, Mom and Michael T. moved to Germany to work for an insurance company which turned out to be a pretty shaky operation. Just when it seemed that things couldn't possibly get any worse, a semi truck rear-ended Dad putting him in the hospital for 2 months. So, Grandmother paid for the three of them to return to the states, 3 suitcases each—all their worldly possessions in their hands. Grandmother picked them up at the Bradenton, FL Greyhound bus station, she on her adult sized tricycle. She financed a small house for them. Mom, Dad and Michael (who was 17 now) all went to work in a mobile home factory at minimum wage and their life started over. Michael joined the Navy. A year later, an old friend secured a job for Dad with the government. Dad came to Western Kentucky working on flood relief and fell in love with the area. They sold the little Florida house, bought the little (6 rooms for rent) motel in Grand Rivers and planned for their eventual retirement, operating this tiny business. But it was Grandmother who helped them secure the financing for this motel. Dad paid her back, you can be sure. It was something that generation did not allow to pass untaken care of, obligations are taken very seriously by pre-baby-boom generations. We are forever grateful to Grandmother for her hand-ups.

Beef Burgundy

3½	pounds lean beef	4	raw carrots, sliced
⅓	cup flour	1	clove garlic, minced
¼	teaspoon pepper		Dash of thyme
2	teaspoons salt	2	cups red cooking wine
6	tablespoons butter	3	slices bacon, half-cooked
3	tablespoons brandy	1	cup sliced mushrooms
3	medium onions, sliced	1	tablespoon tomato paste

Cut meat into 1½-inch cubes. Combine flour, salt and pepper, coat meat cubes with this flour mixture. Melt 4 tablespoons butter in heavy saucepan. Add floured meat. Brown on all sides over very high heat. Pour brandy over meat and set it aflame. Melt remaining 2 tablespoons butter in a separate pan and sauté onions and carrots for 5 minutes (carrots will still be hard). Add onions and carrots to meat mixture. Add garlic and thyme, then red wine and just enough water to cover meat. Add half cooked bacon which has been cut into small pieces. Cover and cook over very low heat, simmering only, for 2½ hours. Add mushrooms and tomato paste, stirring well. Cook 30 minutes longer. May be served over cooked white rice.

10 servings

This recipe submitted by Anita Williamson.

Also, I owe my beginnings in adult life to her as well. While a sophomore in college, I was selected to be one of 80 students from the California State College system to study abroad in Sweden for a year. Well Grandmother had bought a $50 savings bond for each of us four kids when we were born. Eighteen years later it was worth $750. She gave it to me to help pay for my year in Sweden. I know I had made her proud at that point in my life.

There are so many wonderful memories I could write about this stubborn, obstinate, bullheaded grandmother, but there just isn't room or time for them all. I definitely acquired a determined spirit from her and that has served me well in most cases, so the above adjectives are written with admiration and love even though her tough spirit sometimes frustrated the devil out of me.

Another story I must share is this—when the Vietnam War ended, I was accepted back into graduate school in California. When I went to buy my very first house, Grandmother loaned me $1,000 to use as a down payment. I bought the house for $25,000 and fourteen months later sold it for $41,000 after having a sign in the front yard indicating it was for sale for about 10 minutes. I brought the profit back to Kentucky and bought the Thomas Lawson house (a state and national landmark) for $24,500. Thank-you Grandmother—from the entire family—for because of your kindness, we were able to help ourselves. Thanks to your thrifty nature, you had the resources to help. Because of you, there is a happy rest of the story.

Chicken Country Captain

4 chicken breasts, each cut in half
8 chicken legs
3 tablespoons peanut oil
1 large onion, peeled and sliced
2 green bell peppers, sliced
2 cloves garlic, minced
1 (8-ounce) can tomatoes, drained, deseeded, and chopped

Freshly grated nutmeg
1 teaspoon freshly ground pepper
1 teaspoon curry (to taste)
½ teaspoon salt
¼ cup currants
3 cups cooked rice
⅓ cup slivered almonds, toasted
2 tablespoons fresh parsley, minced

Preheat oven to 350°. Brown chicken in the peanut oil over moderate heat. Arrange in baking dish and set aside. Use browning skillet to sauté the onion, peppers, and garlic for about 5 minutes. Add the tomatoes, nutmeg, pepper, curry, and salt. Simmer for another 3 to 4 minutes. Pour the tomato mixture over the chicken and bake covered for 30 minutes. Remove from oven and sprinkle with currants. Return to oven for 15 more minutes. To serve, place ½ cup rice on each plate and top with a piece of breast and chicken leg plus sauce. Garnish with toasted almonds and parsley.

Serves 6 to 8

Chicken Florentine

6 half-breasts of chicken, boned
½ stick of margarine
2 tablespoons oil
2 10-ounce packages frozen chopped spinach
½ cup mayonnaise
Salt and pepper to taste

1 (10¾-ounce) can condensed cream of chicken soup
1 tablespoon lemon juice
1 teaspoon curry powder
½ cup sharp cheese, grated
½ cup cornflake crumbs

Salt and pepper chicken, sauté lightly in margarine and oil for 10 minutes. Cook spinach. Drain or squeeze dry. Spread spinach in bottom of a 2-quart casserole. Top with breasts. Mix mayonnaise, soup, lemon juice and curry. Pour over chicken. Sprinkle with cheese. Top with crumbs.

Bake at 350° for 25 minutes.

Serves 6

This is me. I don't like to talk about me very much, yet I'm very proud of who I am and what I've accomplished in life and what my life is all about. The next cookbook will be more about me, but for now let me say I'm another piece of the original 5 piece picture puzzle (Mom, Dad, Grandmother, Michael Lee and me).

When I got out of the Navy after the war ended—I was an explosive ordnance disposal officer (EOD) (I was trained to disarm bombs ranging from a cannonball to a nuclear weapon) who was truly glad that I never saw combat in Vietnam. Luckily I was stationed on the east coast rather than the west coast.

I'm pictured here as I was traveling (hitch-hiking) across the country with my dog, Stanley after being discharged. I was enjoying the second real break in my life. The first one was three months spent bumming around Hawaii with my best buddy from high school right after we graduated in 1967. This break was between my Navy career and graduate school. I was slim and trim because I had been swimming a mile twice a week and running 5 miles every day as part of my EOD program. I was ready to break out and see the world a little.

I met so many new and wonderful people hitch-hiking. Stanley and I traveled over 15,000 miles and saw 35 states. I had an awful time emotionally with the Vietnam War. I chose EOD as my job in the Navy because I wanted to prevent destruction and death, not be a part of it. I thoroughly enjoyed the open spaces as well as the confinement and strict regimentation of the military. I also thoroughly enjoyed the honor of serving our country and even feel that mandating two years of military service after high school would be a good thing for America. Anyway, back to my story, it was a great three months off.

If I can reflect even more deeply, I'd like to share a life experience with you all that is a major essence of my being. When I was a little boy I always went to church with my mom. Dad wasn't that fond of our form of church going. My sister had other things on her mind. One brother got sick every Sunday so better to leave him home and my littlest brother couldn't be bothered. Oh well, it was Mom and I and it was "our" time together. I had her all to myself. Anyway, I was twelve years old, maybe a little older. Our church had a wall of glass on one side with a tree just outside the window. A little bird, a sparrow I believe as I look back, smashed into the glass and fell to the ground outside, dead so far as I could tell. I was horrified. I have a serious aversion to death and violence. I just sat there. It seems no one saw or experienced this but me. I looked at Mom. She was listening to the sermon. I just couldn't sit there any longer. So, I got up, went outside to pick up the little bird and bring her into the church so everyone could pray for her at the altar. Just as I bent down to pick up the bird, she stood up and flew up to a tree branch just above my head. She proceeded to sing to me, chirp, chirp, chirp. She flew away after another minute or so.

I saw God talk to me for the first time then. I realized he had me witness this act. This event changed my love for life, changed my belief system. It caused me to respond by acting, acting to bring this creature, one of his creations to his altar for his blessing. I saw, I felt God tell me, "son, I have the power over life and over death and it is through my will that I give life to you, and to all others." Just as in Jesus' resurrection, God reached down in front of me and showed me his will and authority.

Well, I went back inside and Mom asked me where I had been. Afterwards, I told her, as I did other friends. They often did not believe my interpretation of this life experience, but that didn't matter to me. I opened my heart and I heard God speak to me for the first time. I believe, therefore I hear, I see, I watch, and I love all along my walk through life knowing it's not often I'm alone.

Canton Chicken

2½ pounds chicken, cut up (or 3 pounds chicken)	¼ cup soy sauce
1 (10-ounce) jar apricot preserves	¼ cup sherry
	¼ cup finely chopped onion

Place chicken in oblong baking dish. Combine remaining ingredients; pour over chicken. Bake at 325° for 1 hour, turning occasionally. Thicken sauce if desired.

Serves 8 to 10

Cola Glazed Ham

10 pounds smoked ham
5 cups cola

1 cup dark brown sugar
Whole cloves

Cover ham with cold water and soak overnight. Heat oven to 350°. Set aside 3 tablespoons of cola. Place ham rind side down in a roasting pan, pour on remaining cola and bake for 2½ hours. Baste frequently. Remove ham from oven and allow to cool for 15 minutes. Remove rind, leaving a ¼ inch thickness of fat. Cut diamond shapes in the fat side and insert cloves in the center of every other diamond. Mix sugar and 3 tablespoons cola; spoon over ham.

Serves 8 to 10

Creamy Pasta Sauce with Fresh Herbs

1½ cups heavy cream
4 tablespoons sweet butter
½ teaspoon salt
⅛ teaspoon grated nutmeg
Pinch of cayenne

¼ cup grated imported Parmesan cheese
1 cup finely chopped mixed fresh herbs (basil, mint, watercress, Italian parsley and chives)

Combine cream, butter, salt, nutmeg and cayenne in a heavy saucepan and simmer for 15 minutes, or sauce is slightly reduced and thickened. Whisk in Parmesan and fresh herbs and simmer for another 5 minutes. Taste and correct seasoning. Serve immediately.

Enough for 1 pound of angel hair pasta, 6 or more portions (2 cups sauce)

Creole Pork Chops

4 pork chops
Onion slices

Bell pepper slices
1 can tomato-rice soup

Arrange onion and pepper slices on pork chops. Mix soup with ½ can water. Pour over chops. Bake in covered pan until tender at 325°. Then remove the cover and bake 5 or 10 minutes more. Quick and good!

Serves 4

Shortly after I got out of the service, I met my partner in life. I won't go into detail here, maybe in my next book. It took all my powers of persuasion to get him to allow the printing of this page. Suffice it to say that he was an answer to my prayers. I was twenty-six years old and had met many wonderful people on my road through life and felt like I had so much love to give to someone yet had no one in my life to receive this love. I had met Mike several months before while he was still in the military. I fell in love even though it was not originally reciprocated. When I returned to Delaware (where he was stationed) after hitch-hiking to and from California, he told me he didn't share my feelings. To make a long story short, I hitch-hiked 3 hours back to Norfolk, VA where I lived. I walked the last 11 miles down the beach to my house. I stopped on the beach a block from my house and looked out to sea in total bewilderment. I prayed to God, "Why, God, why? Why do you give me so much love in my heart and so much love for life and all that it involves, yet give me no one to share it with." A combination of circumstances had led me to a very vulnerable juncture in life.

I prayed and prayed. I cried. I yelled. I kicked the sand. I felt miserable, rejected and depressed. I said, "God, please hear my heart crying out to you. I'm at a point in life where I'm about to take my life. Please, Lord, help me!"

You know, he listened. He picked me up, carried me across the beach, across the road to my house, up the stairs, and he put me to bed. I rested.

It's twenty-five years now that Michael Lee and I have been together. My mother and father felt like they had another son, their favorite son-in-law. They love him. Everyone in the family loves him. Everyone at Patti's loves him. I hope you'll continue reading and love him as we all do. God, thank-you for the greatest gift I could have ever dreamed for. Thank-you for giving me the strength to share this part of our family's story with my old and new friends alike. Thank-you God, for never making me feel I'm ever alone.

Hear, oh God, my prayer:
If I'm ever alone, hear oh Lord my prayer
If I'm ever in doubt, hear oh Lord my prayer
If I'm ever in need, hear oh Lord my prayer

Oh Lord, open our hearts, to speak of our needs,
open our eyes and ears to heed your response

For in our belief we'll never have to walk alone

Eggplant and Ground Beef Casserole

1	pound ground beef	1	teaspoon oregano
2	tablespoons salad oil	1	tablespoons Parmesan cheese
1	medium eggplant	1	cup grated cheddar cheese
⅓	cup flour	1	teaspoon salt
¼	cup olive oil		Pepper to taste
2	cans tomato sauce		

Shape ground beef into thick patties. Season to taste with salt and pepper. Brown in hot oil. Slice eggplant into thick slices, (do not remove skin). Season with salt and pepper, coat with flour, and brown in olive oil. Place cooked eggplant slices in shallow baking dish. Top each with browned meat patties. Cover with tomato sauce. Sprinkle oregano and Parmesan cheese over it all. Top with the grated cheddar cheese. Bake at 300° for 35 minutes.

Serves 6

Fettuccine with Fresh Peas and Ham

2 tablespoons unsalted butter
1 small onion, finely chopped
3 ounces ham, cut into julienne
   strips

1 cup heavy cream
2 cups shelled peas
1 pound fettuccine
Salt

In a large pot bring 5 quarts salted water to a boil. In a frying pan melt the butter over low heat. Add the onion and sauté, stirring frequently, until translucent, about 3 minutes. Add ham and cream. Simmer, stirring frequently, for another 5 minutes. Season to taste with salt and keep warm. Add the peas and pasta to the boiling water and cook until the pasta is al dente. Drain the pasta and peas and arrange them on a warm platter. Pour the cream mixture over the top and toss well. Serve at once.

Serves 6

Ham Tetrazzini

2 cups diced cooked ham
6 tablespoons butter or
   margarine
6 tablespoons flour
2 cups milk
⅛ teaspoon pepper

¼ teaspoon marjoram
½ cup grated sharp cheddar cheese
1 (4-ounce) can mushrooms
2 tablespoons chopped pimento
1 (8-ounce) package spaghetti
1 cup buttered bread crumbs

Melt butter and blend in flour. Add milk, pepper, marjoram and cook until thick. Add cheese and blend. Add mushrooms, pimento and ham. Cook spaghetti in salted water, drain. Put spaghetti in greased casserole and pour ham mixture over it. Sprinkle with bread crumbs. Bake at 350° for 20 to 30 minutes.

Serves 6 to 8

Here we are. This is one of Patti's earliest Christmases. Back in those days we weren't very busy after Thanksgiving, but Dad was home for the holidays. Mike worked at Reed's Rock Quarry during the third shift. Mom waitressed in the evenings and cooked in the mornings. I was the daytime waiter and evening cook. They were harder times than now, but you can see by the smiles, they were great times!

Hamburger Stroganoff

1 pound ground chuck	1 tablespoon tomato paste or
½ pound fresh or canned	catsup
mushrooms, sliced	1 teaspoon Worcestershire sauce
2 small onions, chopped	½ teaspoon salt
3 tablespoons butter	⅛ teaspoon black pepper
2 tablespoons flour	1 cup sour cream
1 can beef consommé	Paprika

Sauté meat, mushrooms and onions in butter. Drain excess fat, sprinkle with flour, stir lightly. Add consommé and stir until smooth and slightly thickened. Add tomato paste, Worcestershire sauce, salt and pepper. Simmer and stir for 10 minutes. Just before serving stir in sour cream. Do not boil. Sprinkle with paprika. Serve over noodles, rice or toasted English Muffins.

Serves 4

Irish Stew

2 pounds stewing lamb or mutton
2 pounds potatoes, sliced
3 onions, sliced
Salt and pepper

2 tablespoons chopped fresh parsley
1 teaspoon chopped fresh thyme
1⅔ cups water

Heat oven to 275°. Trim meat, leaving a little of the fat. Season meat and vegetables with salt, pepper, 2 teaspoon of parsley and the thyme. Layer potatoes, meat and onions in a large casserole. Starting and finishing with a layer of potatoes. Add water and cover tightly. Cook for 2½ hours, shaking occasionally to prevent sticking. Add water if needed, check fairly often. The potatoes will thicken the finished stew so it should not be too runny. Brown top under a hot broiler and sprinkle with remaining parsley.

Serves 6 to 8

Grandma Rose's Lasagna Rice

1 32-ounce jar spaghetti sauce with meat
3 cups cooked rice
1 egg

1 cup cottage cheese
6 ounces mozzarella cheese
¼ cup grated Parmesan cheese

Preheat oven to 350°. Butter 9x13-inch baking dish. Mix egg and cottage cheese. Place rice in dish. Then spread egg mixture over rice. Put meat sauce on top of egg mixture. Sprinkle top with mozzarella cheese. Sprinkle Parmesan cheese over mozzarella cheese. Cook for approximately 30 minutes.

Serves 6 to 8

*"This has been one of my family favorites for years.
It is a great dish for reunions or church dinners."*

This recipe was submitted by Rose Greenlee, February 2000

Sometime later, Michael T. finished his tour of duties overseas and returned to join the family business. Mike's the quiet one. You see him around but he doesn't say much. Just last year, he became president of Patti's Enterprises, LLC and has become a lot more outgoing. When you see him now he looks an awful lot like me and we often confuse our customers because they're talking to the other one of us rather than the one they think they recognize. So, be careful, we're known to have fun that way.

Here he is pictured with his lovely wife, Lawana. They met while she was a hostess at Patti's on the Pier. They now have three lovely children, Arielle, Anna and Adam. I can't say enough about what a wonderful mother she is. She mostly is a six day a week stay at home mom, just like ours was. She takes her kids to piano, dance, gymnastics, violin, cheerleading, etc., etc. And to church every Sunday and Wednesday. Mike along with Lawana's dad (Norvell) built a beautiful home for Lawana and Michael and their family in Kuttawa. Norvell is the head carpenter at Patti's. My brother is a superb father also and as the youngest of four, he got the least attention. So it seems he tries to make up for it by being a good dad at his home. His children simply adore him. I don't envy him, father of three children and security figure to the 250 employees at Patti's. But, I am very proud of him. Someday, as he always seems to follow in my footsteps (older brothers can be good for something), he'll write his cookbook and tell you all more about his family. 'Till then, if you see a me look-a-like pounding on a nail, it's most likely brother dearest.

Lazy Lasagne

1 (16-ounce) package Egg
  Noodles
1 (16-ounce) ricotta or creamed
  cottage cheese
1 cup shredded mozzarella cheese

1 cup grated Parmesan cheese
1 (32-ounce) jar of prepared
  spaghetti sauce
1 pound browned beef, drained,
  add to sauce

Cook noodles according to package directions, drain. Toss noodles with ricotta, mozzarella and Parmesan cheese. In 9x13-inch baking dish, spoon enough sauce to cover bottom. Layer half the noodle mixture and half the sauce, repeat. Bake 25 to 30 minutes in 375° oven.

Serves 6 to 8

Marinated Hot Dogs

2 small cans crushed pineapples
  (do not drain)

1   small jar of apricot preserves
10-12 hot dogs (sliced in bite sizes)

In a large frying pan, heat pineapples with juice and jar of preserves. Add sliced hot dogs. Do not cover and simmer until hot dogs are cooked. Even better made the day before serving!

Serves 8 to 10

Mexicalli Pie

2 packages Martha White Mexican
  Cornbread Mix
2 cups shredded taco cheese
1 pound ground chuck

1 packet taco seasoning
1 small can green chiles
1 small onion, diced
1 small can refried beans

Preheat oven to 325°. Brown ground chuck with the diced onions and green chiles. Drain fat. Add taco seasoning and 1 cup of water. Cook until contents are thickened. Mix cornbread according to package directions. In a medium sized casserole dish, pour ¾ of cornbread mixture. Cover with ground chuck mixture and cheese. Pour remaining cornbread mixture over the top and bake to a golden brown.

This recipe submitted by Mike Costello.

Serves 6 to 8

Hey guys! 3 amigos. The owners, me—the dreamer, Michael T.—the builder, and Michael Lee—the glue that helps hold the rest together. Brothers in so many ways, friends in other ways—each working to make Patti's 1880's Settlement a unique experience for the whole family. Patti's — that "special place to bring that special someone in your life." A place where falling in love is made a little easier.

101

Michael's Fried Peanut Butter & Jelly Sandwich

Your favorite peanut butter
Your favorite jelly

Sandwich bread
Butter or margarine

Warm a skillet. Spread your peanut butter and jelly on the bread and place them together. Lightly butter bread outside and place in skillet. Fry until peanut butter and jelly are melted together and bread is toasted.

"I have loved this sandwich ever since I was a kid. When I was younger, my Mom, Patti, would fix my brothers grilled cheese sandwiches. I didn't like grilled cheese so she started fixing me these fried peanut butter & jelly sandwiches. I still enjoy them today and share them with my kids."

Contributed by Michael Tullar, February 2000.

Mushroom Chicken in Herb Cheese Sauce

¼ **cup butter (½ stick)**
4 **boneless chicken breast halves (about 1⅓ pounds total), skinned**
½ **pound thickly sliced mushrooms**

½ **cup dry white wine**
4 **ounces semi-soft herb cheese**
¼ **teaspoon dried dill-weed**
Salt

Melt butter in medium skillet over medium-high heat. Add chicken and cook until golden brown, about 4 minutes on each side. Transfer to platter using slotted spoon: keep warm. Add mushrooms to skillet and cook until softened, stirring frequently, 4 to 5 minutes. Remove with slotted spoon; sprinkle over chicken. Pour wine into skillet and bring to boil. Add cheese and dill-weed and stir until smooth and slightly thickened. Season with salt. Pour over chicken and serve.

4 servings

In this photo are my sister Roni, her daughter Kim and her grandson Dohnte. They come twice a year to visit and always get put to work. Roni hopes to retire here in the near future. She's more than welcome because sisters, much less such good sisters, are hard to come by. You can tell she's a doll. Look at that smile.

Pasta with Sausage and Peppers

2 pounds sweet Italian sausage

3 tablespoons best-quality olive oil

1 cup finely chopped yellow onions

3 sweet red peppers, stemmed, ribs and seeds removed, cut into medium-size julienne

1 cup dry red wine

1 can Italian plum tomatoes, including the liquid, (2-pounds, 3-ounces)

1 cup water

1 tablespoon dried oregano

1 teaspoon dried thyme

Salt and freshly ground black pepper, to taste

Dried red pepper flakes

1 teaspoon fennel seeds

½ cup chopped Italian parsley

6 garlic cloves, peeled and finely chopped (more if you like)

Prick the sausage links all over with the tines of a fork and put them in a pot with ½ inch water. Heat over medium heat and simmer the sausages, uncovered, in the water for about 20 minutes. Let the pot boil dry and fry the sausages in their own fat. Cook them another 10 minutes, turn occasionally until they are well browned. Remove and drain on paper toweling. Pour sausage fat out of the pot but do not wash pot. Set it over low heat, add the olive oil and onions, and cook them, covered, until tender, about 25 minutes. Add peppers, raise the heat, and cook uncovered for another 5 minutes, stirring often. Add the wine, tomatoes, water, oregano and thyme. Season to taste with salt, black pepper and red pepper flakes. Bring to a boil, reduce heat and simmer, partially covered, for 30 minutes. Slice the sausages into ½-inch thick rounds. When the sauce has simmered for 30 minutes, add sausages and fennel seeds, simmer, uncovered for another 20 minutes. Add parsley and chopped garlic and simmer for another 5 minutes.

Enough for about 2 pounds pasta, (2 quarts sauce)

Serves 10 to 12

This pretty much completes the family as Mom and Dad created it. Notice our brother Craig on the far right. I'm the hippie on the left. Notice how much Mom's and my hair are alike. Of course, Dad has no hair to compare—ha, ha!

What a family—all in all a pretty good one. Sure we have our share of differences. But love, unconditional love conquers all. Mom and Dad let us know they loved each other very, very much. They made us feel that every day. Therefore, we learned to love each other and others every day. They taught us how to be respectful of others. We always answered the phone, "Tullar residence, Chip speaking." We always addressed folks older than us by Mr. or Mrs. We never lied or spoke dirty words growing up or else we placed ourselves in danger of having our dirty mouths cleansed thoroughly with water and a bar of soap. We certainly never back talked to our mother. OH BOY, if we did!

But most importantly, our parents taught us to believe in ourselves, who we were as individuals and who we were as a family so that when hard times came, we'd have the inner strength to buckle down—and overcome.

Quick Brunswick Stew

1 large onion, cut in thin wedges
1 tablespoon vegetable oil
1 (16-ounce) can tomatoes, cut up
1 (16-ounce) can sliced potatoes, drained
1 (12-ounce) can whole kernel corn
1 (10¾-ounce) can condensed tomato soup
1 (8-ounce) can lima beans, drain
2 (5-ounce) cans boned chicken
¼ teaspoon salt
Dash pepper

In large saucepan cook onion in hot oil until tender but not brown. Stir in tomatoes, (do not drain). Add potatoes, not drained corn, soup, limas, salt and pepper. Bring to boil, reduce heat; cover and simmer 10 minutes. Drain and cut up chicken; stir into mixture. Continue cooking until heated through.

Makes 6 servings

Spaghetti Pie

6 ounces spaghetti
2 tablespoons margarine
⅓ cup grated Parmesan cheese
2 well beaten eggs
1 cup cottage cheese
1 pound ground beef or bulk pork sausage
½ cup chopped onion
¼ cup chopped green pepper
1 8-ounce can (1 cup), tomatoes, cut up
1 (6-ounce) can tomato paste
1 teaspoon sugar
1 teaspoon dried oregano, crushed
½ teaspoon garlic salt
½ cup shredded mozzarella cheese (2-ounce)

Cook the spaghetti according to package directions: drain (should be about 3 cups spaghetti). Stir margarine into hot spaghetti. Stir in Parmesan cheese and eggs. Form spaghetti mixture into a "crust" in a buttered 10-inch pie plate. Spread cottage cheese over bottom of spaghetti crust. In skillet cook ground beef or pork sausage, onion, and green pepper. Until vegetables are tender and meat is browned. Drain off excess fat. Stir in undrained tomatoes, tomato paste, sugar, oregano, and garlic salt. Heat through. Turn meat mixture into spaghetti crust. Bake, uncovered, in 350° degree oven for 20 minutes. Sprinkle the mozzarella cheese on top. Bake 5 minutes longer or until cheese melts.

Makes about 6 servings

The photos on this page are a mere snapshot of the memories created with Marian Bauguss, today our most senior employee. Marian came to work at Patti's in 1982 as a waitress and Frank, her wonderful husband, was our first Santa Claus. Marian quickly developed into our dining room manager. Every Thanksgiving we would close at 7 pm, a tradition still today, and start decorating for Christmas so we'd have it ready for our guests by Saturday night. Marian became my biggest helper. Together, we decided to make her our first full time decorator. Today, we start decorating for Christmas the week after labor day with three plus full time decorators working on the inside  of Patti's and four working on the outside building and garden lighting. This all began because of Marian's push to make elaborate decorations a hallmark of Patti's. This aspect of Patti's has made us unique from all other restaurants.

Today, Marian's student, Barbara McAbee follows in Marian's footsteps as well as blazing an even brighter trail. Marian today runs "Reflections—a mirror of memories" here in our settlement. You can see a showcase of her warmth, compassion and love of decorating shared with her co-workers, Sharon Earles and Betty Lou Johnson.

Marian's greatest legacy (besides her enduring love for our family, creation and development of the whole Patti's picture, and spirit of goodness and godliness for all who come into her presence) is her love for the less fortunate children of our area. At the height of her career, she brought over 600 handicapped children to a series of Christmas parties at Patti's. It was the children's most exciting outing of the year. The teachers would say the kids looked more forward to this event than anything else in their year. We both had to put this event aside due to heavy schedules. But, Marian and I both becoming partially retired this year are going to recommit our spirits to the redevelopment of this most honorable of causes. Anybody wishing to help with this series of events during the Christmas holiday season, please talk to Marian at "Reflections". Tell her Chip says to say "hi."

Swiss Steak with Apples and Prunes

6   pieces boneless chuck steak,
    about 3 pounds
Flour
1   tablespoon vegetable oil
1   small onion, finely chopped
½   stalk celery with leaves, finely
    chopped
1   cup beef broth

½   cup strong tea
½   teaspoon salt
¼   teaspoon pepper
¼   teaspoon allspice
¼   teaspoon ground thyme
12 prunes, pitted
3   large apples, peeled, cored, and
    quartered

Dip steaks in flour. In a skillet, quickly sear steaks in vegetable oil over high heat. Add onion and celery to pan as you turn steaks. Transfer steaks and vegetables to a shallow baking dish. In the same skillet, bring broth and tea to a boil, scraping brown bits from the pan, and pour the mixture over the steaks. Add remaining ingredients except apples (if using dried apples, add now), cover, and bake at 350° for 40 minutes. Add fresh apples, re-cover, and cook 20 minutes longer.

Serves 6

Turkey Piccata

1¼ pounds turkey breast cutlets
½   teaspoon salt and ¼ teaspoon
    freshly ground pepper
⅓   cup all-purpose flour
2   tablespoons olive oil, divided

½   cup dry white wine
1   lemon, sliced thin
1   tablespoon butter
Parsley sprigs

Place turkey between 2 sheets of wax paper; pound to ⅛ inch thick. Sprinkle with salt and pepper. Place flour on plate; dip turkey in flour to coat both sides, shaking off excess. Heat 1 tablespoon oil in large skillet over high heat. When hot, add half the turkey and cook until golden, about 1 minute per side. Transfer to serving platter. Add remaining 1 tablespoon oil to skillet and repeat with remaining turkey. Transfer to platter. Add wine and lemons slices to skillet and bring to boil, stirring to scrape up browned bites. Swirl in butter. Pour over turkey and garnish with parsley.

Serves 4

Marian, my dear friend, with all our memories we've shard together, the greatest in my mind will always be the time we prayed together in the gardens when we were about to lose Patti's. You and I talked to our God and he showed me the road to our salvation—the very next day. You, in my mind, will always be a huge reason Patti's 1880's Settlement is here today and this book can be written. I love you and thank you for being my friend and the "old crow" in my life.

Turkey or Chicken Dressing

4   medium onions, chopped
5   stalks celery, medium chopped
⅓ cup bacon drippings
2   cups dry French bread, crust removed, crumbled
2   cups cornbread, crumbled

1   tablespoon sugar
Pepper to taste
3   eggs, beaten
Chicken or turkey broth
1   tablespoon crushed sage

Fry onions and celery in drippings until almost done. Crumble breads together, add all ingredients. Include enough broth to make dressing of pouring consistency. Pour into a baking dish about 3 inches deep and bake until well set and brown on top. Serve with giblet gravy.

Serves about 8

Veal Chops Braised in Wine

4 veal chops or steaks
   (½ to ¾ pound each)
Salt and pepper
2 tablespoons butter
2 tablespoons olive oil

4 green onions, chopped
1 cup dry white wine
2 tablespoons butter
½ cup chicken broth
¼ cup chopped parsley

Salt and pepper the chops generously. Heat olive oil. And butter, brown chops on both sides over medium- high heat. Add chopped onions, wine and broth. Cover and cook over low heat for 1 hour. Remove chops. Swirl 2 tablespoons butter into sauce with a wire whisk and pour over each chop. Sprinkle parsley on top.

Serves 4

Vegetarian Chili

3 cloves garlic, minced
1 tablespoon cooking oil
2 (14½-ounce) cans chunky chili-
   style tomatoes, drained
1 (12-ounce) can beer
1 (8-ounce) can tomato sauce
4 teaspoons chili powder
1 tablespoon fresh oregano or
   1 teaspoon dried oregano,
   crushed
1 tablespoon Dijon-style mustard
1 teaspoon ground cumin

Hot pepper sauce (optional-several
   dashes)
1 (15-ounce) can pinto beans,
   rinsed and drained
1 (15-ounce) can white kidney
   beans, rinsed and drained
1 (15-ounce) can red kidney
   beans, rinsed and drained
1½ cups fresh or frozen whole
   kernel corn
1½ cups chopped zucchini and/or
   yellow summer squash
¾ cup shredded cheddar or
   Monterey Jack cheese (3-ounce)

In a 4-quart Dutch oven cook garlic in hot oil for 30 seconds. Stir in drained tomatoes, beer, 1 cup water, tomato sauce, chili powder, Oregano, mustard, cumin, ¼ teaspoon pepper, and hot pepper sauce if desired. Stir in beans. Bring to boiling; reduce heat. Simmer, covered, 10 minutes. Stir in corn and squash. Simmer, covered 10 minutes more or until vegetables are tender. Top each serving with 2 tablespoons of the shredded cheese.

Makes 6 servings

When growing up, I was four years younger than my sister and she thought of me as a pest, to say the least, a pain in the neck. She considered all three of her brothers nuisances she had to take care of, baby sit, etc. We weren't very close growing up. We are today but we certainly were not back then. Since I've been developing Patti's, I've developed another sister to go with the old one. Her name is Anita Williamson. She is the mother of two very handsome, smart young men, Justin, a Murray State University Freshman and Johnathan, a junior at Marshall County High School. This woman is married to her childhood sweetheart, the dapper Dan Williamson of the Lone Oak Dairyette. A nicer guy you couldn't ask for. Miss Anita is the General Manager of all the Settlement operations. She's Michael T's right hand. She started as a waitress, then Mr. Bill's dining room manager and now head of all operations at the company. She is a great best friend and there is nothing I wouldn't feel comfortable about sharing with her—not that my life isn't an open book anyway. She worked all this time, was a wife, mother and professional woman during the age when there weren't a lot of roads to follow. She created her own and turned trails into roads for her fellow employees to follow—especially other female employees. She has accomplished the almost unheard of in these parts, to become the head of the largest independent restaurant in the region and have two outstanding sons, of whom we are all proud. Anita loves me as I do her—as brother and sister. She is a part of my family and always will be. She will always be an example to the young people at Patti's that hard work, dedication to your family and work do pay off. The sacrifices she made in working so often instead of being with her children were like what my dad did for us while we were growing up. But she's a woman and it shouldn't but it does make a difference. She will continue to be successful because her heart is genuine; firm but genuine. Her word is her honor. Her integrity is unquestionable. The picture I present to you of her is one of my favorites. It reflects her pride, her confidence, her willingness to admit a wrong when wrong. It shows her as the beautiful, smart, loving part of what makes her family and our family so unique—so special. Folks, when you see her, be proud for her. There aren't a lot of women in this area who have walked the rough road she has and come out looking as superb as she has. Thanks for your friendship, Anita.

Love Always,
Patti, Bill, Chip, Michael T.,
Lawana, Michael Lee

Venison Chili

2 pounds ground venison
   (ground sirloin or ground
   round)
1 medium onion, chopped
1 cup celery, chopped
1 green pepper, chopped
Salt and pepper to taste
1 (8-ounce) can tomato sauce

1 (8-ounce) can tomatoes
1 (15-ounce) can chili con carne
1 (16-ounce) can red kidney
   beans
¼ teaspoon garlic powder
1 teaspoon chili powder
½ cup red wine

Brown meat, onion, celery and green pepper. Season with salt and pepper. Drain off all fat. Add remaining ingredients, cook covered for 30 minutes. Simmer uncovered for several hours. Freezes well.

Serves 6 to 8

Venison Roast

2 bay leaves
6 large onions, quartered
6 large potatoes, quartered
1 venison roast, 8 to 10 pounds

2 packages Lipton onion soup
   mix
Margarine
Salt and pepper

Trim venison of all fat, and pierce with a sharp knife in several places. Boil 30 minutes with bay leaves, onions and potatoes. Remove meat, do not wash. Throw away vegetables. Put soup mix in bottom of roasting pan adding enough water to dissolve mix thoroughly. Fill holes in meat with margarine. Salt and pepper generously. Place meat in pan, cover and cook in moderate 325° oven, 30 minutes per pound.

Serves 10 to 14

Employees, friends, family—sometimes the lines blur and
it's hard to tell the difference.

Banana Oatmeal Bread—Medium Loaf

2	cups bread flour	½	cup chopped nuts
1	cup oats	2	tablespoons vegetable oil
1	teaspoon salt	¾	cup mashed bananas
1	tablespoon sugar	½	cup water
1½	teaspoon yeast		

Mix all above together, let rise, knead, let rise again. Grease medium size bread pan. Fill and bake at 350° for 35 to 45 minutes.

Cranberry Nut Bread

4	cups flour		Zest of 2 oranges
1	teaspoon salt	1½	cup orange juice
3	teaspoons baking powder	4	tablespoons melted shortening
1	teaspoon soda	2	eggs, well beaten
2	cups sugar	2	cups chopped pecans
2	cups raw cranberries, coarsely ground		

Sift together flour, salt, soda, baking powder and sugar. Add to nuts and cranberries, beating in eggs, orange rind and juice, then melted shortening. Add to dry ingredients. Mix well. Pour into greased and floured loaf pans. Bake 1 hour at 350°.

Makes 2 loaves

1st row: Jan, Chip, Debbie, Sabrina, Jennifer
2nd row: Deannie, Anita, Lisa, Deena Gail, Dad
3rd row: Marian, Jill

This is a perfect example of how the family is growing. This photo is of the group that worked to entertain handicapped children at Christmas over at Mr. Bill's dining area.

Just to mention a few success stories: Debbie and her husband, Mike, opened a pizza parlor here in Grand Rivers and it is going strong; Deannie now co-manages Miss Patti's Iron Kettle restaurant; Anita is our general manager for all operations; Lisa is our head dining room manager; Marian is a primary gift shop manager.

I'm so proud of all these people and of our company. We almost always promote from within and encourage people to grow and improve and to find fulfillment and happiness.

Easy Cream Cheese Danish

2 (5½ ounce) packages biscuit mix
3½ tablespoons sugar
⅔ cup milk

⅓ cup butter or margarine, melted
    (5⅓ tablespoons)
Cream cheese filling (see recipe below)
Powdered sugar glaze

Prepare cream cheese filling. In a bowl, combine biscuit mix and sugar. Stir in milk and butter until blended. Drop dough by rounded tablespoonfuls onto lightly greased cookie sheets to form 16 mounds. Make a shallow well in center of each using the back of a spoon. Place 1 heaping tablespoon cream cheese filling into each well. Bake at 425° for 12 to 15 minutes, or until golden brown. Cool 5 minutes, drizzle with glaze. Serve warm.

Makes 16 pastries

Cream Cheese Filling

2 (3-ounce) packages cream cheese
3 tablespoons sugar

1 egg
4 teaspoons flour

In a small bowl, combine softened cream cheese and sugar. Beat in egg, then flour. Beat until smooth.

Powdered Sugar Glaze

1 cup powdered sugar
1 tablespoon warm water

¼ teaspoon vanilla

Combine and mix well until smooth.

Our first Christmas
with the Glasgow
side of our family.

All together, a group photo of people from Patti's 1880's, Patti's
of Glasgow and Patti's on the Pier.

Our first Christmas
with the Patti's on
the Pier family.

Easy Onion Bread

1	large Spanish onion, thinly sliced	½	teaspoon salt
¼	cup butter or margarine	2	tablespoons butter or margarine, melted
4	eggs	½	cup milk
1½	cups sour cream	1¾	cups biscuit mix
1	teaspoon caraway seed (optional)		

Sauté onion in ¼ cup butter 10 minutes or until golden brown. Set aside. Slightly beat 3 eggs; add onion, sour cream, caraway seeds and salt. Stir well and set aside. Combine 2 tablespoons butter, 1 egg, and milk; stir well. Add to biscuit mix, and stir just until moistened (dough will be slightly lumpy. Spread dough in a lightly greased 12x8x2-inch, baking pan. Spread onion mixture over dough. Bake bread at 375° for 30 minutes or until top is set.

10 to 12 servings

Mexican Cornbread

1½	cups self rising cornmeal	1	small can cream style corn
1	cup milk	3	fresh jalapeño peppers, chopped
⅔	cup oil	2	cups shredded sharp cheddar cheese
3	eggs		

Mix all ingredients together and pour into a 10-12-inch skillet. Bake 375° for 45 minutes to 1 hour or until brown. Let set and cool for a least 15 minutes before cutting.

Quick Rolls

2	cups of your favorite baking mix	1	stick margarine or butter, melted
1	cup sour cream		

Melt margarine, and mix all ingredients together. Bake in greased muffin tins at 450° for 15 minutes.

Makes 6 to 8 servings

Let me introduce Mr. Frank Flynn and his lovely wife, Marilyn. They are Patti's very best customers. They come every Sunday and have been coming for years and years. Frank is our present day historian. He has taken a mutitude of the pictures you see in this book. It's special people like the Flynns that make us all feel that what we do is worthwhile. It's so nice to be loved and appreciated and we love and appreciate them so much in return. They also are my father's best friends. Thanks so much for your friendship and support. Love to you both.

My good friend, Bob McLean and his lovely wife, Liz, the carousel pole spinning broad that she is, are two very special friends. Folks, Bob moved here from California after reading Rand McNally's designation of Murray as the best place in America to retire. He found me and talked me into allowing him to develop a brochure for Patti's in 1991 and has helped me create all the printed material for our company in the last decade. He isn't going to be able to do this cookbook, since he recently found out he has serious vision problems that can't be corrected. So here's to you, a glass of cheer, a wink of the eye—now you and Liz are both forever a part of us.

Pear-Pecan Muffins

1½ cups boiling water
¼ pound dried pears
2 cups flour
2 teaspoons baking powder
½ teaspoon baking soda
½ teaspoon salt

2 eggs, beaten
¾ cup sugar
⅓ cup unsalted butter, melted
½ cup chopped toasted pecans
½ cup chopped candied ginger

Pour boiling water over the pears. Let stand for 15 minutes. Drain well, reserving ½ cup of the liquid. Cut pears into ½-inch pieces, set aside. Preheat oven to 400, butter muffin tins. Mix together flour, baking powder, baking soda and salt. Set aside. Blend together the reserved pear liquid, eggs, sugar and melted butter until smooth. Stir in pears, pecans and ginger. Add the combined dry ingredients. Stir until just blended. Spoon into buttered muffin tins, ¾-inch full. Bake until center is firm, about 20 minutes. Cool 5 minutes, then remove from tin.

Makes about 12 regular size muffins

Spoon Bread

1 pint sweet milk
½ cup meal
½ teaspoon salt

3 eggs, well beaten
½ teaspoon baking powder

Heat milk to nearly boiling. Stir in meal gradually and cook until like mush. Add baking powder, salt and eggs. Pour in greased casserole. Bake 30 minutes at 350°. Dip from casserole with large serving spoon. This is a side dish to be served with dinner. Top with butter.

Our most famous photo to date.

"Thanks always, Bob."

Rolls

½ cup shortening
½ cup sugar
1 cup scalded milk
2 beaten eggs

1 cake yeast
¼ cup lukewarm water
1 teaspoon salt
4 cups flour

Combine shortening, sugar and salt in scalded milk.

Dissolve yeast in water. Add yeast to cooled milk mixture, then beaten eggs. Stir in sifted flour. Let set in refrigerator at least overnight. Flour board and pin, roll out and cut. Dip in butter. Let rise 2 hours. Bake at 375° until golden brown on top.

Makes 10 rolls

Sweet Potato Biscuits

1 cup mashed cooked sweet
    potatoes
3 tablespoons unsalted butter,
    melted and cooled

1 teaspoon sugar
1 cup all-purpose flour
2 teaspoons baking powder
½ teaspoon salt

Combine sweet potatoes and 1½ tablespoons of the butter and stir in sugar. Sift together the flour, baking powder, and salt. Add the mixture to the sweet potato mixture. Stir the dough until it is just combined. Roll the dough out ½-inch thick on a floured surface. Cut out biscuits with a 2-inch round cutter. Arrange them on a buttered baking sheet. Brush the biscuits with the remaining 1½ tablespoons butter. Bake in a preheated 375° oven for 20 minutes, or until they are lightly browned.

Makes about 10 biscuits

After our first year, we opened up the walls connecting two of the motel rooms and made the restaurant's family room. It's right behind the hostess station. The window behind Greg and Kent Northcutt is where you usually sit while waiting to be seated. One night Greg and Kent set up to play folk songs. It was a great atmosphere they created. Finding this photo reminded me of another story. Greg and Kent belonged to a youth group at the Calvert City Baptist Church. Every Sunday evening of our first 2 years in business (Hamburger Patti's Ice Cream Parlor), the kids would drive over about 8:30 pm after their evening meeting. There were about 20 of them, sometimes more, sometimes less. Well, this was always more business than we'd had all day and we could barely handle the volume. The kids all pitched in helping us get everyone served. They'd get their own drinks, some would help cook, some would help serve, some would dip ice cream. They often filled our whole top dining room.

These were some great young people. Greg became an attorney, Terri became a doctor (she was Mom's doctor throughout her battle with Lou Gehrig's disease), Sheri and Debbie Low both worked with us at Patti's and are now doing a fine job of raising their own families. How remarkable to think these kids grew up to take care of us. That always makes me so proud. Every time I go to Paducah, I drive past Dr. Terri Telle's office and smile.

Patti Tullar and Patti's won't fade from memory very soon just like these kids have never faded from ours. These kids now have their own families. How many will bring their children to Patti's? I hope they stop me and introduce themselves and say hi. It most surely will bring warmth to my heart and a glow to my soul. God bless to all those kids who were there with us during those first few months of business. You'll never know how much you all meant to Mom, Dad and I— you were the high point of our week.

Walnut Bread

½   cup sugar
1¼ cup milk
1   egg

3   cups biscuit mix
1   cup walnuts

Mix together sugar, egg, milk, and walnuts. Add biscuit mix. Beat hard for 30 seconds. Spread in well greased and floured loaf pan. Bake at 350° for 45-50 minutes. Cool on rack before cutting.

Whipping Cream Biscuits

1¾ cups self-rising flour

½   pint whipping cream

Preheat oven to 450°. Measure flour into medium mixing bowl. Make a hole in center and add whipping cream. Blend with fork until mixture forms a ball. Roll on floured board to ¼-inch thickness and cut out biscuits with small biscuit-cutter. Bake for 10 to 12 minutes.

Makes about 12 biscuits

Zucchini-Pineapple Bread

3   cups all-purpose flour
2   teaspoons soda
1   teaspoon salt
½   teaspoon baking powder
1½ teaspoons cinnamon
¾   cup pecans

3   eggs, beaten
2   cups sugar
1   cup oil
2   teaspoons vanilla
2   cups shredded zucchini
1   3-ounce can crushed pineapple, drained

Combine all dry ingredients, including nuts. Beat eggs; add pineapple and zucchini. Fold in dry ingredients and hand beat for two minutes. Bake 30 minutes in two loaves or one tube cake pan at 350°.

Mrs. Gail McQuigg—our very first manager—and she was a cracker-jack manager. Remember, there were only about five of us the first couple of years. We had very few employees, we certainly didn't need many. Mom, myself, Michael Lee, Dad, Edna Hooks (who owns the Grand Rivers Fish Market across the street now) and just a couple others who worked part time were all we needed the first two or three years. But Gail took us to a higher plateau with her degree in Home Economics. She was the driving force that carried us forward in a big way. And she's an excellent cook!!

Dad, Mom, me, Gail, Michael Lee and David Wentworth as Santa.

Barbecued Limas

2	cups dried lima beans	1	teaspoon salt
1	onion, chopped	1½	teaspoons chili powder
¼	cup meat drippings	1	can condensed tomato soup
¼	pound salt pork, in strips	5	tablespoons vinegar
1½	tablespoons prepared mustard	¼	pound salt pork, diced
2	teaspoons Worcestershire sauce		

Soak Lima beans overnight, drain. Add enough water to cover beans, and the salt pork, diced. Cook over medium heat until tender. Then drain the beans, but save the liquor. Brown the onion (a minced bud of garlic is good also) in the meat drippings. Add all of the ingredients except the limas and pork, cook for 5 minutes. Place the beans in a greased casserole, pour the sauce over them. Top with salt pork strips, and bake at 350° for 30 minutes. If beans get dried out, add the bean liquor, little by little.

Beef, Eggplant and Cheese Casserole

1	large unpeeled eggplant, cut into ½-inch thick slices	½	pound smoke sausage (may omit)
4	slices bacon	2	cups canned tomatoes
1	large green pepper, chopped	3	tablespoons tomato paste
1	large onion, chopped	2	teaspoons garlic salt
1	garlic clove, chopped	1	teaspoon oregano
2	pounds top round of beef	½	teaspoon pepper, fresh if possible
			Parmesan cheese, grated

Cut eggplant and cook in boiling, salted water for 5 minutes. Drain and reserve them. In a large skillet, cook bacon until crisp. Drain and reserve them. In the fat remaining in pan, sauté pepper, onion, and garlic, until onion is transparent. Add beef, sausage and brown lightly, stirring with fork. Add tomatoes, tomato paste, garlic salt, oregano and pepper. Mix 2 tablespoons each of flour and water and stir the paste into the meat. Arrange half the eggplant slices in a casserole, add half the meat mixture. Sprinkle lightly wit h cheese. Repeat the layers, finishing with a heavy layer of cheese. Bake the casserole in a 350° oven for 30 minutes. Serve with bacon crumbled on top. Freezes well.

Patsy Smith was our first employee to move through the ranks to the position of general manager. She started out as a server and when we opened our restaurant in Glasgow, we needed a strong person to run the show in my absence. She was a love. Her son, Michael, would come to the restaurant from school and study at a table in the family room while his mother worked. He graduated from Livingston County High School as the Valedictorian and went on to college. Patsy's husband, Paul, was our first carpenter. No more likable person will you ever find than Paul.

Patsy, Michael and Paul bought the Cumberland House Seafood Buffet restaurant in Kuttawa and ran it quite successfully for several years before retiring in Orlando, Florida. For years, Orlando had been their twice yearly vacation destination.

As you can see, she was a lovely lady of many faces and talents. Hey—look Patsy—there's my lamp. Is the tag still underneath it?

Thanks for the memories.

127

Chicken and Dressing Casserole

1 cup celery, chopped	1 large loaf of bread, cubed (or use ½ corn bread and ½ loaf bread)
1 large onion, chopped	
1½ teaspoons salt	
1 teaspoon sage	3 eggs
2 tablespoons poultry seasoning	3 cups chopped cooked chicken
	3 cups chicken gravy

Combine celery, onion, seasonings and bread cubes and mix well. Stir in eggs. Layer dressing, then chicken in a large buttered casserole. Pour gravy (chicken stock thickened with 3 tablespoons cornstarch) over top. Cover and bake at 350° for I hour.

Serves 6

Chicken Spaghetti Casserole

1 cup cooked spaghetti	¼ cup butter, melted
2 cups diced chicken	¼ cup green pepper
1 cup cheddar cheese, grated	2 tablespoons pimento
1 can mushroom soup	3 eggs, beaten
½ cup chicken broth	1 small can mushrooms

Mix all together. Pour into a lightly greased casserole container. Cook 45 minutes at 350°.

Serves 6 to 8

Hominy Pudding

3 eggs, beaten well	1 pint milk, scalded
3 cups canned yellow hominy	Salt and pepper to taste

Place drained hominy in a food processor, chop to medium. Beat eggs and add milk. Add hominy, salt and pepper. Pour into well-buttered casserole and bake at 350° until firm, about 40 minutes.

Serves 6

Dixie Eggs

4   hard boiled eggs
2   tablespoons chopped green pepper

⅓   cup (¼ pound) pimiento cheese

Make white sauce of:
3   tablespoons butter
4   tablespoons flour
2   cups milk

1   teaspoon salt
¼   teaspoon paprika

Add green pepper and cheese to white sauce and cook slowly until cheese is melted. Add sliced eggs and pour into buttered casserole. Mix crumbs and butter to cover the top. Bake 25 minutes at 325°.

Serves 6

Italian Noodle Casserole

Meat Mixture
1   pound ground beef
1   tablespoon salad oil
1   clove garlic, minced
1   tablespoon parsley flakes

1   tablespoon basil
2   teaspoons salt
1   can (2½ cups) tomatoes
1   (6-ounce) can tomato sauce

Cheese Mixture
2   (12-ounce) cartons large curd
    cream style cottage cheese
2   beaten eggs
2   teaspoons salt
½   teaspoon pepper

2   tablespoons parsley flakes
½   cup grated Parmesan cheese
1   (10-ounce) package wide
    noodles
1   pound mozzarella cheese or
    American cheese, sliced very thin

Brown ground beef in salad oil and drain. Add remaining Meat Mixture ingredients. Simmer uncovered until thick, about 1 hour. Cook noodles in boiling salted water until tender, drain, rinse in cold water. Mix Cheese Mixture ingredients except mozzarella or American cheese.

To Assemble:
Place half the noodles in 13x9x2-inch baking dish. Spread half of the cheese mixture over the noodles. Add half the sliced cheese and half the meat mixture. Repeat layers. Bake in moderate oven, 375° for 30 minutes.

Serves about 8 to 10

Here, Jack Reynolds shares a laugh with some friends.

I'd like to tell you a story about this old fart (his personal favorite nickname) of a man. He was my grandmother's best friend during her tenure in our gift shop. He operated his LBL photo studio gift shop in one area of the original gift store while Grandmother operated the rest of the gift store. They had dinner almost every night together and the two of them were the biggest rabble rousers. They stirred up stuff, if you know what I mean. They laughed and schemed all the time. They poked fun at themselves and all the rest of us as well. They made each other's day! When Grandmother died, a part of Jack did as well. He eventually retired and just recently passed away himself. We miss them both. The entire world will miss his fabulous pictures of the Land Between the Lakes. He might very well have been the area's most gifted photo artist. He was an old friend of Patti's as is his lovely wife Betty.

Their son, Jack, Jr., now operates a business in town, Kentucky Kayak Kountry which offers kayaking trips down a nearby river.

Old South Hominy

3	tablespoons butter	1½	cups milk
3	tablespoons flour	1	cup chopped ripe olives
1	small onion, grated	½	cup grated cheddar cheese
½	chopped green pepper	1	#2 can white hominy
½	teaspoon dry mustard		Bread crumbs

Melt butter and cook onion and pepper 5 minutes over low heat. Add flour, mustard, salt to taste, and milk. Cook until thickened. Add cheese, olives, and hominy. Place in casserole dish. Cover with crumbs and bake until it bubbles.

Add a can of large mushrooms, coarsely chopped, for an extra treat.

6 servings

Pork Chop Casserole

6	pork chops	½ soup can of milk
2	onions, sliced	Vegetable oil
2	potatoes, peeled and sliced	Salt and pepper
1	can cream of mushroom soup	

Brown pork chops and onions in a small amount of oil. Season with salt and pepper. In an 8x12-inch greased baking dish, layer chops, half the onions, potato slices and remaining onions. Combine soup and milk and pour over casserole. Cover with foil. Bake at 350° for 1½ hours. If desired, remove foil and top with 1 cup grated cheese last 5 minutes of baking.

6 servings

Pictured here is me in the center with John Pat McReynolds to the right of me. John Pat was our first gift shop manager and started with the company in Grandmother's 91st year. He helped us begin improving the quality of merchandise we offered our guests. This was a huge step for us. You see, Grandmother didn't like changes—imagine that. Which of us doesn't get more settled in our ways as we get older. Grandmother was no exception and John Pat with his outstanding sense of humor, was able to guide us through this first growth stage. He and Grandmother worked together until just prior to Grandmother's death.

Wherever you are, my friend, please remember you'll always be the first in Patti's retail history as your sister Gail was the first manager the restaurant ever had. A special thanks to you both.

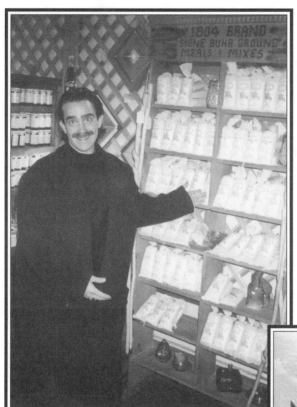

At left: Tim Timmons, the son of Dwight and Norma Timmons.

Ladies, let me introduce you to Tim Timmons of "Dwight's" ladies apparel, shoes and gifts in Paducah. Tim's customers in Paducah included all those of influence and high social standing. He also counted my mother as one of his customers. There's nothing Patti loved better than beautiful clothes and accessories. I'll never forget the first time Mom took me to Tim's store

which his mother, Norma, helped him operate. We walked in and there was my long time acquaintance, Tim. He gave Mom a big smile (his trademark) and a huge hug hello—then introduced me to his lovely mom. Well, it was early December and Mother was putting Christmas gift ideas (her wish list) into my head. She pointed out this $450 purse, then the gloves to match, then the wallet to match, then the eyeglass case to match and then more things to round out the entire ensemble.

I choked..... "Mother, what do you need a $450 purse for?"
She replied, "But I'll love it the rest of my life."
I said, "It's nice."

Soon, thank goodness, we left and climbed back into the car where I shared with her a small dose of reality by letting her know we were not wealthy and she did not need to keep up with those in Paducah who were. I gently led her to the understanding that ours was a very small business and still in something of a struggling phase.

Well, she was not pleased. We drove about four blocks to the public library where she got out to return some books (Mother was a voracious reader) and there on the seat was the purse.

'My Lord,' I thought to myself. She already has the purse. She wants to make sure we get her the other pieces. When she returned, I just shook my head and said, "Mother, you are a character." We laughed and laughed.

Before she died, she gave the purse to my sister who will, I'm sure, cherish it till the day she dies. I wouldn't be at all surprised if at that point it has enough life left to be passed on to her daughter. It truly is a beautiful purse, simple but made in such a way that you just know it will last forever. Tim carried high quality merchandise.

But the lesson here is that our family believes that if you want something—then believe in yourself and make it happen. And to date, that philosophy is why we are where we are. We are driven. We push ourselves. We are goal oriented. If you want to accomplish something, guess what? There's only one way to get it done and that's to start working on it—right now! When that's accomplished, establish a new set of goals and get to it.

That leads me to a second thought. If you work as hard and as consistently as my mother always did, you must take time to reward yourself for your hard work. Without some reward, large or small, the work becomes drudgery. There's balance to this. If you spend more than you earn, you'll go under. If you work so hard that you don't allow yourself to enjoy the fruits of your labors, you'll burn out and your work will run amuck. Anyway, Mom felt she deserved the purse and how could I argue? She worked awfully hard.

Now for the rest of the story. Tim and Norma fell on some difficult times and had to close the store. Norma and Mom were friends and Mom asked me if I'd consider hiring Norma to work in our gift shop (we only had one shop at this point in our history). So, I drove down to visit the store and spoke with Norma. She asked me to please talk with Tim because he was having a horrible time with the store closing. He had withdrawn completely. I agreed to talk with Tim and we set up an appointment to spend some time together.

He came to Grand Rivers to meet with me. In no time, our acquaintance status progressed to close friendship. My heart went out to him. Life is so unfair for many of us at times. I found in Tim a chance to help someone who was willing to help himself. Tim moved to Grand Rivers and became our gift shop manager. He oversaw the first major expansion of our retail division.

I had never been to market before. This is where we go to find merchandise for all of our stores. Tim showed me the ropes. He took me and Mother shopping together for our new gift lines and it was a marvelous experience. He was a wealth of knowledge. Ladies, Tim was a strikingly handsome man. With large dark eyes; huge, warm, genuine smile; smooth easygoing charm; nothing but love in his heart; impeccable taste and true dedication to his work; I developed a great admiration for Tim, the man. The ladies who shopped the store (men don't really shop, you know), all the other employees and our family, of course, loved Tim to death.

Shortly after coming to Patti's, Tim became ill with a terminal illness. His suffering broke all hearts. Tim spent 2 weeks in the hospital during the final construction phase of our gift shop expansion. With $40,000 worth of new merchandise coming in—much of it in boxes already all over the place—Tim checked himself out of the hospital and worked 24 hours almost continuously directing us as to the display and placement of every item. Pictured on the previous page, you see him pointing to his success. Tim was with us for another year and during this time, he discovered how to be happy with himself. He had always looked beyond himself for someone else to make him happy but we helped him to understand that you have to love and respect and appreciate yourself before you'll find real happiness. If you look for it in others, they can take it away from you and leave you standing naked.

When Tim died at his home here in Grand Rivers, he had some of his friends from Patti's with him. It was, by his own admission, the happiest he had been in his life. When most of us went to his funeral, he wasn't there. He's already gone to Key West where he and Mother today are riding in a rickshaw having a great time. I truly look forward to our meeting again some day. Thanks Tim for moving us to the next level in our retail development.

Just a closing note—one of Tim's best friends was Marjorie Rea. Today, she lives in his house. I really believe life does work out in direct proportion to what good you do while living it.

Sausage Casserole

1 pound sausage	2 packages dry chicken noodle soup
1 bunch celery	½ cup uncooked rice
1 onion, chopped	5 cups boiling water

Brown sausage and drain. Chop entire celery bunch, including leaves, and mix with rice, soup and onion. Place everything into 9x13-inch casserole dish. Pour five cups of boiling water over all. Bake at 350° covered, 1½ hours and an extra ½ hour uncovered.

Makes 8 to 10 servings. May be frozen.

Squash Casserole

2 pounds fresh squash, cooked and drained	1 onion, grated and squeezed to remove some moisture
1 stick butter	1 carrot, grated
1 can cream of chicken soup	1 cup sour cream
1 package herb stuffing	

Put ⅓ of stuffing aside; combine ⅔ stuffing with rest of ingredients. Put layer of stuffing on bottom of large casserole dish and fill with rest of mixture. Put layer of stuffing on top. Bake at 350° for 30 minutes.

Serves 8 to 10

Turnip Casserole

1½ pounds turnips, peeled and thinly sliced	2 tablespoons flour
2 tablespoons butter	1 cup milk
1 onion, thinly sliced	½ cup grated cheese, good with sharp cheddar
⅔ cup chopped green pepper	Salt and pepper
⅓ cup chopped celery	3 tablespoons bread crumbs

Cook turnips until just tender. Drain, sauté in butter with pepper, onion, celery. Add flour and milk. Stir in cheese, put in casserole dish. Top with bread crumbs. Bake in 350° oven until bubbly and brown.

Serves 8 to 10

Baked Cinnamon Apples

6 cups green apples, peeled, cored, and cut in eighths
1 cup sugar
2 teaspoons cinnamon
½ teaspoon freshly grated nutmeg
2 tablespoons apple brandy
Juice of 1 lemon
4 tablespoons melted butter
Sour cream, optional

Mix thoroughly apples, sugar, cinnamon, and nutmeg, using your hands. Put into a casserole dish and sprinkle with brandy, lemon juice, and melted butter. Cover and bake in a preheated 375° oven for 35 to 45 minutes, or until apples are soft. Can be cooked ahead and reheated. Serve hot or warm with sour cream if you wish.

Serves 8 to 10

Egg A-La Martin

Make a cream sauce of one tablespoon of butter, one tablespoon flour and a cup of cream or milk. Season with salt and red pepper. When it begins to thicken add two tablespoons of grated cheese. Break into this four or five eggs slightly beaten. Cook until the eggs are done which will take a very few minutes. Or you can pour the cream sauce in a baking dish, sprinkle the cheese over it then drop the eggs in whole. Cook until the cheese is melted and the eggs set.

Eggs New Orleans

2½ cups tomatoes
1 small onion
½ green pepper, chopped
1 teaspoon sugar
¾ cup bread crumbs
¼ cup celery, chopped
8 eggs
½ cup American cheese
Salt, pepper and bay leaf

Cook tomatoes, pepper, onion and seasoning for 10 minutes. Remove bay leaf. Add bread crumbs. Place in casserole. Break eggs on top and sprinkle with salt and pepper. Cover with cheese. Bake in a moderate oven 350°, until eggs are set and cheese has melted.

Serves 8

Eggs à La Suisse

2 ounces Swiss cheese, thinly
    sliced
4 eggs, room temperature
4 teaspoons freshly grated
    Parmesan cheese

Salt
Cayenne pepper
¼ cup half and half
½ cup shredded Swiss cheese
Freshly grated nutmeg

Preheat oven to 350°. Fill roasting pan with ½ inch water and place in oven. Divide sliced cheese among 4 custard cups. Break 1 egg into each cup. Sprinkle with Parmesan, salt and cayenne

Spoon 1 tablespoon half and half over each. Sprinkle with Swiss cheese and nutmeg. Place cups in roasting pan. Bake until cheese melts and eggs are set, 15 to 18 minutes. Remove cups from water and dry carefully. Serve hot.

4 servings

Brunch Frittata

1 tablespoon cooking oil
1 cup fresh or frozen broccoli
    florets
½ large red sweet pepper, seeded
    and thinly sliced
¼ cup chopped onion
½ teaspoon dried Italian
    seasoning, crushed

¼ teaspoon salt
⅛ teaspoon pepper
10 beaten eggs
2 tablespoons milk
2 tablespoons finely shredded
    Parmesan cheese

In a 10-inch skillet, broiler proof, heat oil over medium heat. Add broccoli, sweet pepper, onion, Italian seasoning, salt, and pepper. Cook and stir until florets are crisp-tender, about 4 minutes, fresh or 5 minutes frozen.

In a medium mixing bowl stir together eggs and milk. Pour over vegetable mixture. As the eggs begin to set, run a spatula around the edge of the skillet, lifting the egg mixture to allow the uncooked portions to flow underneath. Continue cooking and lifting edges until eggs are nearly set (moist surface). Remove skillet from heat: sprinkle with cheese. Broil 4 to 5 inches from heat for 1 or 2 minutes or until top is just set. To serve, cut into wedges.

Makes 6 main servings

Then along came Miss Ellen Pratt. After Tim left us, there was a huge void in all our lives. We started interviewing folks for the job. We just couldn't find anyone who energized us the way Tim did. Then this young lady dressed in a white linen suit with matching hat interviewed. She came from Dillards Department Store. She hadn't any buying experience but was dazzling in her class and charm, much the way Tim had been. And like Tim, she was fun. She wanted more out of her life than she already had (always a plus when interviewing to find someone working to improve him or her self).

While I walked her around Patti's and out to her car, a Saab, I realized that this is who I wanted. I could train her how to buy gifts and she could teach me the systems that big companies like Dillards already used. It would be a good fit.

Ellen was fortunate (or unfortunate) enough to be at Patti's to oversee the largest expansion our retail division ever saw and the largest retail expansion in Grand Rivers since Thomas Lawson developed the town in 1890. She oversaw the developmental start of Patti's 1880's Settlement. We went from one store attached to Patti's to three stores when the Settlement came into being. I'll never forget the hours of hard work this lady put in and the hours of talking we did developing everything. It was a great match. We grew together so much which is a key in my management philosophy. It's not important as an owner or manager for you to know everything. Encourage your people to teach you as well as you teach them. Encourage an environment which fosters personal and professional growth and you will get more out of your employees, which in turn, teaches you more.

Ellen, I discovered, had this beautiful, strong exterior but her natural confidence level underneath the shell was weaker than you'd expect. For no reason. She is quite a capable person. But this is quite often a fault in many successful people, including myself. I think it actually is a check in our personal checks and balances system. It keeps us from being too full of ourselves and attempting foolish endeavors.

However, in business, the ability to finish a task is in direct proportion to how focused we are. Low self-esteem tends to make us focus more on our insecurities than is actually necessary. This, in turn, prevents us from focusing on the goals and tasks that are important. We all have to work to sort of ignore our insecurities in order to maintain a high level of achievement. This is a lesson I learned from Ellen.

During our year together, Ellen and I worked hard on her learning how to deal with that fluctuation in her and my personalities.

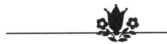

Ellen married John while at Patti's and soon the two of them were off to a new start in Texas. I watched a champion of greatness walk away. I haven't seen Ellen in years but I know somewhere out there is a person who when she slows down even for a while, will think of Patti's and get a twinkle in her eye. I certainly get that twinkle thinking of her. You know, I can't put my finger on it—why, after all these years and thousands of employees, why I remember what Ellen was wearing and what she was driving. It may be because God sent me an angel—no, Tim sent me an angel with God's help. As a matter of fact, I believe the spirit spends some time with us here on earth after a person dies and I asked Tim before he died to send me the perfect replacement for him. I'm sure he sent Ellen.

Jesus arose on the third day and then appeared before his disciples. I feel that our lives are much like his and we, too, have the ability to communicate to each other after death for a time before we actually go on to our after-life. I've always believed that Patti's was a gift from God for the people of God, so that those who are willing to slow down enough to experience it could feel God's love as they walk the paths and enjoy the gardens. We just have to be receptive. We have to focus. We have to believe.

Just like my bird story, I believed, therefore the experience was for me—to others it wouldn't have been the same. I believed in Tim's ability and his relationship with God, which allowed him to send Ellen to us. In one way or another, I'd like to think that each employee has been sent to us at Patti's with God's purpose driving the outcome. Ellen and thousands others have worked as one to build Patti's into what it is today and what it is evolving into. Believe in your dreams. They can happen, but you must believe.

I'd like to give you another case in point. When we started building Patti's 1880's Settlement, Republic Bank had given us $100,000 towards the $600,000 it was going to lend us to build our first phase. So we started to build. Then, at the last minute, someone in Louisville's main office canceled the deal. And there we were....$200,000 in bills due in 30 days, $2,000 in the bank, a partially completed Settlement and no way to finish the project, much less pay the bills we'd already incurred.

After 11 banks all said, "NO" to loaning us the money to finish the Settlement which we had started. I was lost. It wasn't that we couldn't cash flow the debt. It was the fact that they didn't believe that large an investment in our tiny town at KY Lake was wise. Grand Rivers was developing very, very slowly. Our successes weren't terribly impressive to date. They were small success stories. Louisville bankers just didn't believe in me and my dream is what it boils down to.

I sat at a table in the gardens with my friend, Marian (Reflections, Grandma, the old crow) and actually cried. I was about to lose everything, but most importantly, I felt I had failed in the Lord's eyes. I thought I had done something that wasn't what he wanted and he was unhappy with me. I was terribly upset. Marian and I held hands and prayed together for the Lord to hear our prayers for help, for guidance, for understanding. I walked away confident that I would find the way. I knew this was what the Lord wanted me to do. I knew it was the others' shortsightedness that caused them not to see. I felt what it must have been like for Jesus, wandering the Earth trying to do good and being faced with the scorn of the powerful. It must have been awful for him and his followers that the Romans couldn't see who he was and the good he embodied; couldn't share in his vision of a better world and better life for all.

Well, I went to bed that night and said my prayers again as is usual. When I woke up the next morning, a light went off in my head. If our company had won the 1st runner up for the Small Business Administration's Kentucky business of the year award, surely we ought to be able to get funding for this project. So I got on the phone and called the Kentucky director of the SBA in Louisville and explained the problem to him and he stated that the SBA could and would guarantee the loan up to $750,000.

Needless to say, 3 days later the first bank I called arranged the funding for the whole project and the rest of the story awaits your perusal in downtown Grand Rivers. There's no doubt in my mind that the Lord set off that light bulb in my little pea brain. He heard and answered our prayer. I was wrong for just a little while. He was actually pleased with what we were doing just as my gut had told me all along. That's why I know if you come to Patti's you'll find a place where prayer is made a little easier. God is omnipresent. His church is everywhere. We try to capture the spirit of peace here for all to experience for a while. I believe in God.

Thanks, Tim, for sending us Ellen. Hope you and Mom are having a great time together.

Grits Patties

⅓ cup uncooked regular grits
2 tablespoons self-rising flour
¼ teaspoon salt

⅛ teaspoon pepper
1 egg, slightly beaten
Hot vegetable oil for frying

Cook grits according to package directions. Stir in flour, salt, pepper and egg. Mix well. Drop mixture by tablespoonfuls into hot oil. Gently flatten with spatula. Brown on both sides; drain on paper towels. Serve immediately.

Serves about 8

Mike's Breakfast Pie

1 pound bacon
1½ pounds frozen hash browns
¾ cup diced peppers (green, red, or yellow)
¾ cup diced tomatoes
1½ dozen eggs

¾ cup milk
1 medium onion, diced
Package Classic Melts, (Kraft, 4 cheeses), grated or your favorite cheeses
1 cup diced ham

Fry 5 slices bacon, save grease. Cook rest of bacon until crisp. Place potatoes in bottom of 12-inch oven safe skillet (with lid). Brown hash browns using grease from 5 slices of bacon. Cook hash browns until just brown. When done press hash browns firmly into bottom of skillet to form a crust. Remove from heat, crumble the 5 slices of bacon evenly over top of hash browns. Spread vegetables evenly over hash brown crust. Whip eggs with milk, salt and pepper to taste. Layer chopped ham and remainder of cooked crumbled bacon over mixture. Pour ½ of milk and egg mixture over ham and bacon. Layer cheese over egg mixture, vary amount to suit your tastes. Pour remaining egg mixture evenly over cheese. Preheat oven to 400°, cook covered for 30 minutes. Then finish cooking, uncovered for 30 minutes. Test with table knife in center, it will cone out clean when done. Sprinkle with paprika and serve in wedges like quiche.

Serves 6 to 8

This recipe may be altered to suit your taste.
Suggestion: Spinach, mushrooms, sausage (pre cooked and drained),
sliced water chestnuts, diced artichoke hearts, pimento or olives, different
cheeses. Just be sure added ingredients are not too juicy.

This recipe was submitted by Mike Flatt.

Phyllo-Wrapped Spinach Rolls

1 tablespoon olive oil
½ cup chopped onion
1 10-ounce package frozen
 chopped spinach, thawed,
 squeezed dry
8 ounces cottage cheese

4 ounces cream cheese
4 ounces crumbled feta cheese
1 small egg, beaten
12 phyllo pastry sheets
1 cup butter, melted (2 sticks)

Heat oil in large skillet over medium-high heat. Add onion and sauté until translucent, about 3 minutes. Reduce heat to low and add spinach. Slowly stir in cheeses until well blended. Cook 5 minutes. Remove from heat. Add egg and mix well. Butter 13x18-inch baking sheet. Stack 3 phyllo sheets on damp towel. Brush each sheet with melted butter. Spoon about ½ cup filling into 1 ½-inch-wide strip down long edge of phyllo. Roll up as for jelly roll, starting at long edge with filling and using towel as aid. Transfer to prepared baking sheet, arranging seam side down. Brush with melted butter. Repeat with remaining phyllo for 3 more rolls. Freeze 15 minutes. Preheat oven to 350°. Cut rolls into 1-inch pieces. Bake until golden brown, 15 minutes.

Makes 72

Strata

4 cups dry bread cubes or crumbs
1 pound bulk sausage, browned
 and drained
½ cup green pepper, minced
1 cup green onions, slices
8 eggs, beaten
4 cups milk

1 pound sharp cheddar cheese,
 grated
2 teaspoons ground mustard
½ teaspoon Worcestershire sauce
¼ teaspoon paprika
8 bacon slices, fried crisp, drained
 and crumbled

Butter a 9x13-inch baking dish. Sprinkle bread cubes evenly over bottom. Sprinkle cooked sausage over crumbs. Place pepper and onions over sausage. Mix eggs, milk, cheese, mustard, Worcestershire and paprika. Pour over sausage. Sprinkle bacon over top. Cover and refrigerate over night. Bake uncovered at 350° for 50 to 60 minutes.

Serves 12 to 15

After Ellen left, the lovelies, Laurie McWilliams, Marla Stone and Karen Ballard became Patti's first ladies of retail. They oversaw the transition of our retail division from a $250,000 a year operation to an $800,000 a year operation. We grew from three stores to five under their watchful eyes. They had help along the way from the wise and witty Marian (Reflections, Grandma, old crow). They all interviewed and truly were each so unique in their strengths that I just couldn't decide which not to hire, so I hired all three. They were a great team. This is Karen in the photo on the left.

Here you see pictured from the left: Anita Williamson (now our general manager), Laurie McWilliams, Mom, Marla Stone, Ellen (on her last buying trip with us), Marian and Lisa Galusha (now our overall dining room manager).

We were on the three new gift shop manager's first buying trip. Karen is missing from this photo so she rated her own picture, on the previous page. This was Ellen's last and she and I were trying to teach the new girls how to shop for our stores. On this particular trip, the girls found a hat shop and all were sporting the latest in haberdashery. The girls had a mission. Take $350,000 and spend it in seven days. This takes grueling 12 hour work days with hardly a break at a water fountain, much less lunch. You really have to like to shop or you'll say, "forget it". These girls really like to shop.

I learned early on that the more women you took with you, the more opinions you heard on what the chances were that a piece of merchandise would be a seller or a dud. It has proved to be a very valuable tool in building the retail side of our business. Today, sales are approaching $1,400,000 which is a long way from Grandmother's first little shop. I hope she's proud of the foundation she laid for us and is looking down with a wry grin. Laurie, Karen and Marla have moved on to other endeavors.

It's funny how life leads us sometimes. Laurie went into business for herself across the street from Patti's at Sew Cool Stuff and opened her second store on Broadway in Paducah. She calls it Sew Cool Two. Marla has married a young man she met at Patti's, John Lujan. He was a waiter. We must have about 15 couples who worked together at Patti's over the years, fell in love and married. As far as I know, all are still together except maybe one couple. That's a pretty good success rate in this day and age. Marla now has a little one at home, Cody. Karen is living and working in Atlanta with a young man named Rob, a sales representative she met on a buying trip. Oh well, one chapter closes and another begins.

Whole Wheat Pecan Waffles

1	cup unsifted whole wheat flour	½	teaspoon salt
1¼	cups unsifted all-purpose flour	2	eggs
½	cup finely chopped pecans or natural almonds	2	tablespoons butter or margarine, melted
1	tablespoon granulated sugar	1¼	cups milk
3	teaspoons baking powder		

Stir together flour, nuts, sugar, baking powder, and salt. Separate eggs. Place whites in a small bowl. Add yolks to flour mixture along with butter and milk. Stir just until dry ingredients are moistened. Heat well-seasoned cast iron waffle maker according to manufacturer's instructions. Beat egg whites until stiff but not dry. Fold into batter. Bake according to manufacturer's instructions. Serve with butter and syrup.

Makes 4 waffles

Above you see Connie Parsons, Peggy Snyder,
Betty Lou Johnson, Dottie Robertson, and Betty Jenson.

Today, the retail division of Patti's 1880's Settlement is run by these people—wonderful folks. It is their job to purchase, organize and sell all the gifts we bring for your enjoyment while visiting our most unique and beautiful collection of retail stores. More about all of them next time. Suffice it to say that these people are all terrific!

Dottie, Michael
Glover and Connie

Bloody Lucy

3 cups tomato juice
2¼ cups sauterne

⅓ cup lemon juice
1 lemon, sliced

Mix tomato juice, sauterne, and lemon juice in a pitcher. Divide among 6 stemmed goblets. Add ice and garnish with lemon slices.

6 servings

Cranberry Tea

1 bag cranberries
2 quarts water
2 cups water
2 cups sugar

3 cinnamon sticks
2 cups orange juice
4 tablespoons lemon juice

Boil cranberries in 2 quarts water until cranberries burst. Strain and discard berries. Add remaining ingredients and simmer 20 minutes. Good served hot or cold. Keeps several weeks in refrigerator.

6 servings

Hot Spiced Tea Mix

½ cup instant tea
2 cups Tang
1 package dry lemonade mix

½ teaspoon ground cloves
½ teaspoon cinnamon
2 cups sugar

Mix thoroughly and store in jar. To make a cup of tea add 2 to 3 teaspoons of mix to 1 cup boiling water. Store in a dry place, tightly covered.

Bette Jensen and Doug Cole are pictured above. Bette is one of our most senior employees. We won't tell you her age but I guarantee you she doesn't show it or act it. Bette handles our shipping and receiving department which is a huge task. She goes to market as one of our buyers and keeps track of our purchase orders. Folks, I'd like to make a point; your life is as good as you feel it is. Bette is a fulltime employee with great responsibility at a time in life when many people are retired. Senior citizens are many of Patti's most stable, dependable, capable and intelligent employees so don't sell yourself short on self-worth just because you're getting older. Remember, my grandmother was 94 before she stopped working, and then it was only because she had health problems that necessitated a move into a nursing home.

Doug Cole is a kitchen supervisor, full time college student (working on his master's) and soon to become father with a great young lady (Amy Burnett) he met when she was a server at Patti's. Another couple that met, fell in love and tied the knot because Patti's brought them together. This always brings me great joy. Even my brother met his lovely wife at Patti's on the Pier. Doug has been with Patti's 7 years as of this writing and is the greatest charbroiler we've ever had. He's the man when it comes to steaks and pork chops. If you've had one of these at Patti's there is an excellent chance that Doug cooked it for you.

Mint Drink

1 jar mint jelly (10-ounce)
3 cups boiling water
1 cup pineapple juice

1 cup orange juice
½ cup lemon juice
12 ounces ginger ale

Boil jelly in water until dissolved. Let cool, add other juices, then just before serving add ginger ale. Pour over ice.

Mint Fruit Tea

2 long stems of mint
Grated rind of ½ lemon
Grated rind of ½ orange
4 tea bags (or 2 tablespoons loose tea)

2 cups boiling water
⅓ cup sugar
3¾ cups cold water
Juice of ½ orange
Juice of ½ lemon

Combine stems of mint, grated rinds, and tea in a heat-proof pitcher or teapot. Pour 2 cups boiling water over all. Steep 10 minutes. Put remaining ingredients in a large pitcher or jar. Strain steeped tea mixture into it and blend. Cool and pour into tall glasses of ice. Garnish with thin slices of lemon or orange and sprigs of mint.

Summer Refresher

2½ cups cranberry juice
1½ cups pink grapefruit juice

¾ cup lemon lime soda or ginger ale, chilled

Combine in pitcher; stir to blend. Serve over ice and garnish with orange or lemon slices.

Many years ago, there were two gentlemen eating at table #14 in the family room. Michael Lee and I started talking with them and discovered that they had recently bought a house on Lake Barkley and moved to Kentucky from St. Louis. They had opened an antique shop in Calvert City. After talking, we discovered that David (pictured above) had recently left his position as an accountant for a huge, multinational construction company. It wasn't too long before David came on board as Patti's first in-house accountant. He and Fred also moved their antique store to a building that once stood where Mr. Bill's is today. Eventually, David left Patti's and moved his and Fred's business to the country store building near Patti's (the corner of Commerce Ave. and JH O'Bryan Ave.) which is where he sits in the photo above.

David eventually moved his antique business back to St. Louis. This gave Mark and Sherri Newcomb the opportunity to buy the building and open an antique mall. But things did not work out in St. Louis for David and he has now returned to our area. David steered Patti's through a period of enormous growth and he did it with a steady hand. For that, I'll always be grateful. Today, he, I and Kay Alexander (my present in-house accountant) are business partners in two dance clubs located in Paducah; Ginger and Pickles and The Pride Factory.

We always maintained our friendship. Unfortunately, David lost Fred years ago, but he and Michael Lee and I are great running buddies. We have very similar interests and travel well together.

Patti's on the Pier is the large building in the center and rear of the above photo. Located in Green Turtle Bay, the beautiful resort in Grand Rivers that sits on Lake Barkley, Patti's on the Pier developed in four years, a name and reputation that nearly eclipsed that of Patti's 1880's.

When Mr. Bill Gary first came looking at our town, he stated that if we wouldn't open a restaurant in this building built on pilings overlooking what was then Port Ken Bar, he wouldn't buy the marina. Well, I knew we needed new ownership of what should have always been the jewel of Grand Rivers. I wanted to own that marina so badly I could taste it. To make a long story short, we spent four years running The Pier at the ever growing and improving Green Turtle Bay. Today it is called The Commonwealth Yacht Club and is a private club.

Mr. Gary has overseen the redevelopment of this beautiful resort on Lake Barkley and has made it into one of the premier resort-marinas between Chicago and the Gulf coast. Great job Bill and family!!!

Mr. Jim Farrell was dining room manager at Patti's on the Pier. Lawana was a young, 18 year old hostess and my brother, Michael T. was general manager and head cook/charbroiler. Mom was the head baker there. Patti's on the Pier had the most beautiful brunch you could imagine. Here, Jim shows off his Easter basket full of colored eggs for the little ones. It was at The Pier where mother made her bowl cakes so famous. Mom's angel food cakes cooled upside down on top of a Coke bottle and one day this bottle fell over on the counter and her cake collapsed. Mom, who never wasted a thing (she grew up during the great depression) put the broken cake into a bowl with; jelly, peanut butter, chocolate syrup, frosting or any other sweet she could lay her hands on. Everyone loved her creation so much that they kept asking her, "What is this?" Her reply, "A bowl cake."

We still serve bowl cakes at Miss Patti's Iron Kettle. Jim, Mike and I are still friends and even though we don't see each other as often as we should, we see him from time to time in Nashville and there's always e-mail.

Pictured at right is Patsy Smith (the first employee to rise from waitress to general manager) and her A+ student son, Michael. They are standing in front of Patti's on the Pier here.

Miss Jan came to me at Patti's of Glasgow and asked for a job. She's the only person I've ever told, "No, you are over-qualified." I wouldn't give her a job because she has two bachelors degrees and a masters and I really thought she'd never be satisfied working in my restaurant. She kept coming back trying to land a job with Patti's. I finally agreed and boy am I glad. She is a jewel if there ever was one. Our relationship has lasted 14 years now and she was another one who married someone she met at Patti's. We had Patti's of Glasgow from 1984 until 1988 and when we closed it, she came to live with Michael Lee and me at our house in Grand Rivers.

She has been our kitchen manager, a gift shop manager, a catering manager, and a hostess. Miss Jan is fabulous. She's a perfectionist. Her dashing and dapper husband (this place is full of charmers), Mr. Brad Cross is her chief assistant and a he's a Godsend for our kitchen at Miss Patti's Iron Kettle.

Jan and Brad are as loving a couple as there ever was. I was honored to be Brad's best man at their wedding. It was truly one of my greatest honors. I hope I lived up to the task. They are still like lovebirds on a honeymoon after years and years, so maybe I did OK.

Jimma, the redheaded Grimm; waitress, then dining room manager at Patti's on the Pier is pictured here. She followed me to Glasgow to be my dining room manager there.

The Glasgow venture is another adventure in high finance. A man came to me and told me he knew of this wonderful building in Glasgow, KY which would make a beautiful Patti's. He worked for an investment firm and he hoped we could work together to build a franchise to make into a multi-unit operation. He had high hopes and his enthusiasm caught on with me.

Anyway, he told me we could expect $100,000 of seed money to get this operation off the ground and then he'd work with me to develop the systems necessary to build a chain of restaurants. We shook hands on the deal. So, I set off to build this new enterprise thinking I could reward my most dedicated employees with great advancement opportunities in the near future. That's a lovely idea, don't you think?

Well, I committed to opening the restaurant and spent a huge amount of money on it, but this individual never came up with the money. It turns out, he was operating on his own behalf, not as an agent of the investment firm. But he never let me in on that little tidbit of information. Another lesson hard learned!

ALWAYS GET IT IN WRITING

AND THEN

RUN IT BY THE MOST COMPETENT ATTORNEY AROUND

I also learned another lesson. Every mistake, no matter how costly, has value. The value is that a mistake is a lesson. It makes you wiser. It builds character. It develops maturity. And it prevents you from making the same mistake in the future when the consequences could be much more drastic or costly. After that, I really understood this lesson I'd heard my dad repeat so many times.

Anyway, on our way home from Patti's of Glasgow, I was going 95 mph (I was really mad at allowing myself to be taken that way) and a State Trooper pulled me over and gave me a ticket. Grimm was with me and looked over and stated most matter-of-factly, "If I'd been driving, we never would have gotten that ticket, you know." I noticed she was in something of a seductive pose and realized that she was probably right. She was (and in her late 40's still is) an absolutely gorgeous woman.

Six months later, Jimma and Dee Dee (who you'll meet shortly) had a flat tire and ran off into a corn field. They were in the same car (Jimma's Nissan 280 Z sportscar which definitely matched Jimma's spirit). The two drove with the flat tire to a little country store. Well, it wasn't the flat that caused them to end up in a corn field. It was a night out on the town. The two of them were great party animals for a short while and a formidable pair in a singles club. A state trooper politely took them home and told them to be careful. No ticket. No warning. Nothing. Yep, she had a way with the fellas and her terrific looks make a difference wherever she goes.

There are hundreds of stories I could tell on Jimma (mostly with Dee Dee in tow) but suffice it to say I truly miss her and always enjoy when she comes home to visit from Fort Walton Beach, Florida.

This is one of my favorite of all pictures. If looks could kill it's obvious one of us is about to be killed. Actually, let me introduce Dee Dee or Delores Schubert. We actually are discussing who loves each other more......yeah. When Patti's of Glasgow took over the building that was L'auberge des Champs, a very fine French restaurant, the one employee who was recommended as a must hire was Dee Dee. She was recently divorced and a mother to 2 teenagers. She was determined to be just fine in the tough world single mothers have to endure. We were soon best of friends.

We've been apart now since 1988 when Patti's of Glasgow closed after three years of struggling to make it work. Those three years were probably the most memorable each of us had during our lifetime. We became friends, buddies, soul mates. Our lives were so out of sorts what with her divorce and the trials of raising two teenagers by herself and finding her way in the world again after 20 years as a housewife and with my trials as the one who had placed this strain on myself and my family and my business not to mention being away from home 5 to 7 days a week. We were soul searching together.

I can say without reservation that I've never had a friend quite like Dee Dee. We grew together to be like a mother and father team to all the kids who became the Patti's of Glasgow staff. We kept the spirit alive for the most beautiful restaurant facility in Kentucky. We built memories and we shared life together; my car that we nicknamed The Mayonnaise Jar, she saw her first drag queen, her first night in a bar as a single person, and many other firsts. 'Thumper', I'd call her because she'd cross her legs, point the toe of her shoe and start thumping the foot remaining on the floor. She was like a bird dog on point sometimes and you'd know she had spotted a man, Robedo. And then there was Angie (her daughter) standing at the end of the Glasgow airport runway, an expert marksman threatening to shoot her mother and her date out of the sky as she was being whisked off in a private plane to Nashville for dinner (the date of a lifetime for this country girl). God made a wonderful woman in Dee Dee; so complex, so shy, so easy to tease.

Every day we'd walk 3 or 4 miles, sometimes more if it wasn't going to be a busy evening. We'd walk together as friends, dear friends and co-workers. And when all was said and done and I had to decide whether to close Patti's of Glasgow or keep it open, I looked at Dee Dee and asked if it was OK to close. I wanted to go home. Would she be OK? I know she knew I missed my home, my Michael, my family, my kids at Patti's. And they all missed me. She looked into my eyes and we each began to cry. It was over.

We knew Patti's of Glasgow needed to close. For us; her second divorce, my first. But this time we were both stronger because of each other and our time together. Dee Dee, and to all that we shared together, thanks for the memories. Joyce, Ernest, Jean Marie, Shawn, Joe Harlan and the rest of the Glasgow gang— I'll never forget you and I hope this picture of Dee Dee and I will help you not to forget me/us and all that Patti's of Glasgow was.

One of many weddings at Patti's of Glasgow — the tradition continues at Patti's Grand River.

It's a bird, it's a plane——yes it's a plane just going over our heads. Fly high, Mr. Toad, fly high. And don't forget to read "The Pokey Little Puppy" to the grandkids—and before you know it to the great-grandkids. Tom, take care of her for me, OK?

At left is Tom, the new man in Dee Dee's life. And a great guy he is, and a damned lucky one, too. Pictured is Tom, Dee Dee and Miss Joyce who was our other running buddy during the Glasgow years.

After closing Patti's on the Pier and Patti's of Glasgow, we decided to concentrate our efforts in downtown Grand Rivers by expanding Patti's 1880's. My father, Bill, called himself "Mr. Patti" for years and it seemed like time to do something about that. So when we built a restaurant catering to tour operators and families, we named it after him, Mr. Bill's. We gave him back his own identity. Mr. Bill's became home to numerous cartoon characters to reflect our theme, created by Mr. Bob McLean, our wizard camera man. We were going to specialize in chicken, fish and ribs—all meats generally served intact on the bone—therefore we called it Mr. Bill's Bone Box.

We had coloring books, song books and entertainment provided by a local lady who had actually played piano on paddle-wheel showboats, Miss Pearl. It was like an old saloon. All the kids working the dining room wore elaborate saloon girl costumes. It was a ball. We all sang. The old upright Steinway piano, Miss Pearl decked out in feathers, pearls and all, we had a blast and if I might say so, we were great.

Tragedy struck during our second week open for business. Miss Pearl suffered a crippling stroke and so came a quick end to everything Mr. Bill's had been built around, the talents of Miss Pearl. We were all devastated. It was 2 years before Miss Pearl played again even for a few songs. We love you, Miss Pearl.

So, we began our second season with Stan and Jan Miles, a wonderful husband and wife team. He played their electronic organ (which could provide the sounds of a full orchestra if that's what you wanted) while Jan sang. What talent those two brought with them to Grand Rivers. Stan and Jan could work the crowd like a couple of Las Vegas pros. They sang and danced, the staff sang and danced the youngsters who came for the show, sang and danced. The show was definitely on again. The pay was not so good yet, so Stan worked during the day in our office, our first Guy Friday to help keep the office staff happy. You always left the office smiling because of Stan's great, upbeat personality. He never had a bad day. But Stan had a history of health problems we never expected him to encounter again.

One morning, he came in to work, clocked in, started up the stairs to the office. The Lord clocked him out. With a heart attack right there at work, Stan was called to the great show in heaven. I'm sure he's playing his electronic organ in God's orchestra. Jan and her children, Alex, Jodi and Angie, all worked at the restaurant. This truly is a family place. Alex is soon to be married and has one of my favorite pieces of art, a photograph of a Jesus look-alike sitting in the front row of a church—sound asleep. I think it's great, even if it is a little irreverent toward organized religion which I'm not opposed to at all. Then there's Angie who recently married Bill Gary IV who is taking over the reins of Green Turtle Bay from his father. Angie's back in Grand Rivers again. And Jodi works in the offices at Green Turtle Bay now. Oh yea, Jodi married Ben who was a busboy at Patti's when they met. Jodi was a server at the time. It's fun watching everyone grow up. And Jan is happily remarried and living in Michigan.

Best wishes to the whole family. Thanks always for being the first real musical group at Patti's. Don't give up on me. I will regrow the musical division some-day as well. I want you to be proud, Miss Jan.

Presenting, from the left: Laura, Michael Lee, Lawana, Miss Jan, Alan, Angie, Sabrina——the Mr. Bill players—quite a fun group.

Above, you see Marcus Baker, a waiter at Patti's, who we commissioned to paint a folk art rendition of Grand Rivers, an amalgam of how it was in the past, how it was at the time the mural was painted, and how it might look in the future. Remember, ours is only a tiny, tiny town. Well, the picture was so large, he painted it under a tree outside in the backyard on stretched canvas. We carried it in and attached it to a wall later. Here, Marcus is standing in front of his work which still hangs very proudly in the main dining room at Mr. Bill's.

Christmas Punch

1 large can pineapple juice
1 cup lemon juice
1 large package raspberry Kool-
Aid

2 cups sugar
½ gallon water

Mix all ingredients. Pour over ice.

Serves 25

Martha Bloodworth—Mother's first baking buddy. No telling how many pots of bread or how many pies those two cooked between them. If they'd have written down just a few of the tales they experienced at Patti's over the years—BOY OH BOY!!!!

Martha retired after 16 years with us. Thanks sweetheart—we miss you. Say hi to Vicki Garrett for us if you ever see her.

I'd like to introduce you all to Mrs. Pat Long (on the left) and Mrs. Lisa Galusha (on the right). Miss Pat loved me so much——and I should stop here, but you know as wordy as I am, I can't. Miss Pat first came to Patti's about 10 years ago. She struggled with diabetes and its terrible debilitating effects but as her health permitted, she worked in our gift shops, did inventory, took reservations and at Christmas when the restaurant was closed, answered our telephones and sold gift certificate to those souls who waited until the last minute to finish up their shopping. Pat Long and Miss Mary Hansen always took care of the place when the rest of us were out starting our Christmas shopping. We all loved her. She was an inspiration because like Stan Miles, she never had a bad day.

I don't think I had a better friend than Miss Pat when it came to taking up for my family when someone would think or speak unkindly of us. I never had to watch my back, no sir. She was my pit bull. I'll never forget a couple of days before she passed away, which was the middle of 1999. I went to see her at the nursing home and I asked if she felt like getting out and going for a ride. She replied, "Anywhere with you, sweetie." She always called me her sweetie and I wheeled her over to my big, new, bright red pickup truck. After a delightful lunch at The Iron Kettle, I took her over to The Settlement and placed the truck in 4 wheel drive. We rode all around the undeveloped part of The Settlement where I

explained the dreams we had for future growth. We rode around a little more and then returned to the nursing home. As I was wheeling her back to her room, she asked me to do her one last favor. She asked me to give the service at her funeral. I did, of course, with great pride in our friendship. I hope I did her proud. See you again some day, girlfriend.

Then, there's Mrs. Lisa Galusha, her last name was McKinney when she started with us fresh out of high school. She's now the mother of two young men, Zack who is 6 and Ryan who is 2. She's married to the handsome Chris Galusha. She has been with us for about 14 years now. She earned her bachelor's degree from Murray State and worked her way up to dining room manager. Lisa is our backbone of the whole dining room operation at Patti's & Bills, folks—she keeps it all together! She is a major contributor to the smooth operation of Patti's along with her assistants Mike Costello and Chris Hatfield. She is a terrific person; cool, calm, collected, intuitive, intelligent, kind, fair, dedicated, tireless, understanding and also very pretty. She's a friend to all and has been promised the general manager's job if and when we open a lodging facility. She wants to be the innkeeper at Patti's if such a job opens up. She'd be great at it and she deserves it.

Here she is pictured receiving one of her many awards. Have fun and enjoy life girl. You are a great mother and wife. Chris, you are a lucky man. Lisa, you too are blessed. Good luck with those two boys. I'm sure their teenage years will be déjà vu for Chris.

Here's Miss Barbara Cross (Brad's twin sister—Jan's sister-in-law), my dad and Mary Hansen (who you'll hear lots about later). This is Barbara's story. I met Babs when she was trying to sell me a newspaper ad about 14 years ago. I don't much believe in advertising per se. I think if you concentrate your efforts and resources on doing your job in excellent fashion, the word of mouth advertising will work for you. Spend the money on improving your customers' experience rather than funding mass media. This is still our philosophy. Anyway, Barbara asked me if I'd like to go water skiing and I'd never been invited anywhere since I lived here (all we ever did was work), so I said, "sure." Well, a couple hours later we were streaking (literally) down the lake having a ball and that's just the beginning of this story.

She eventually became the "hostess from hell" at Patti's because she would not be pressured. Most customers have no idea how difficult the host position is at Patti's. Getting 500 to 600 people seated on time from 3:30 pm to 10:00 pm when some are late, some are early, some arrive with more, some arrive with fewer, some have had a few cocktails, some say they have reservations when we're pretty sure they don't, etc., etc., etc.

Well, Barbara could handle the pressure. She ran the seating charts at Patti's for years and very well, I might add. No offense ladies, but Barbara had her PMS days and Lord have mercy on those who crossed her on those days. She'd look over the top of her reading spectacles and glare! She was a sight to behold, as she stood her ground. God love her—the rest of us do.

Then came the terrible accident one winter night. She was driving home out in the country where she lives. She fell asleep at the wheel going about 35 miles an hour and her car left the road and hit a tree head on. She was nearly killed. After walking a mile to her house to get help, all she could do was complain about ruining her horse coat that she had bought at Ashleigh's Boutique. She told everyone, paramedics, nurses, doctors—everybody—for 2 days when we didn't know whether she'd live or die. I thought this would make a good commercial for our clothing lines.

After spending months in the hospital enduring surgery after surgery, Barbara is put back together again, our bionic woman. She's getting married this year (2000) and having her reception at Patti's. And she has a new horse coat from Ashleigh's. Oh, so many stories—but let me end with this one.

Barbara has found the Lord. She has dedicated her life to telling stories, witnessing about the Lord. I've asked her to write a story about the love there is for everyone at Patti's. I know it will be a good story and one that constantly evolves. It's nice to have her still working, even if indirectly, with all of us again. God bless your life together, Barbara and David.

Halloween with another extraordinary hostess: Melissa Baker with her buddy Angie Turner

Audrea was one of our very first Hostesses back in the very early 80's.

Two hostesses and a cook: Marjorie Rea, Doris Thomas, and Beth Ann Smith

Could You Please Repeat That?

In case you're confused as to what the hostess REALLY says when you are seated at Patti's, we've included one version of the hostess speech.

"Hello, I'd like to welcome you to Patti's. We're famous for our bread, baked in clay flower pots and served with both whipped regular and strawberry butter.

Our house specialty is our pork chop. Each chop is two inches thick, charbroiled with our own special seasoning and weighs about a pound.

All of our dinner entrees come with your choice of soup or salad. We have a spinach salad with hot bacon dressing, a garden salad with your choice of dressing.....or the soup of the day of which we have two. You also have your choice of steak fries or baked potato with your dinner.

If you'd like appetizers before your meal, we have mozzarella cheese sticks (they are really cheese logs) dipped in a beer batter and deep fried. We also have deep fried dill pickle chips that have been rolled in a cracker meal batter. My favorite is our homemade potato chips served loaded with chili and cheese, diced tomato and diced green onion.

Last, but the most tempting of all, we have our homemade pies. Our mile-high meringue pies are made with eighteen egg whites. For the chocolate lover, we have Bill's Boatsinker Pie. This is a gooey chocolate brownie base drizzled with chocolate syrup, coffee ice cream drizzled with chocolate syrup, whipped topping drizzled with chocolate syrup and all finished off with a maraschino cherry. We have about 14 other homemade pies to choose from. Your server will tell you about them after dinner, so save room.

Enjoy your dinner. Your server will be right out."

Cider

1 gallon cider	1 teaspoon allspice
1 cup brown sugar	1 stick cinnamon
1 teaspoon whole cloves	1 pinch nutmeg

Mix ingredients together and heat thoroughly.

Please meet Miss Kay Alexander. Kay is responsible for all the accounting functions at Patti's. This task alone warrants me sharing a personal point of achievement. Our company, in 24 years has never neglected to pay a bill on time. Our credit is impeccable. We guard this just as we guard our integrity and reputation. Kay is responsible for making sure our financial integrity remains intact.

Kay started at Patti's as a fry cook. That's right, a fry cook in the kitchen. When our accounting position came open after Kay's predecessor took a position with Martin Marietta, Kay applied for the job. I could hardly believe it, but she had the desire to better herself and little did I know, she had experience. She said what she didn't know, she'd teach herself. Well, my sister-in-law, who knows the books and computers said she'd teach Kay and the rest is history.

Kay's trusted staff includes Becky Morris in accounts payable and accounts receivable and Robin Allen in payroll. They are close friends and comrades in arms. Again a model for success, we promoted from within as we do whenever possible, believing in people who believe in themselves. This is a great way to find and superb way to keep outstanding staff.

Folks, I'd like to introduce Miss Deannie Norman to you. Deannie came to Patti's many, many years ago from the Executive Inn. She started as a waitress and became a dining room manager and after a long period of time moved to Louisville to be closer to her three children who had all migrated there. After several years in Louisville, she moved back to Western Kentucky with Rod, the new man in her life. We found out she was back. It turned out that we had an opening she might be interested in. Now, she is co-manager (with Darnell) of our Iron Kettle restaurant just down the street from Patti's. Without going into great detail, let me state for the record that she's a jewel. Her heart is pure gold as is her soul. Look her up to say hi next time you're in the Kettle.

Another Halloween favorite is Miss Renee Systo. Renee has just left us (April of 2000) after about 15 years. We'll miss her greatly. Here, friendly Freddy is about to silence her wicked ways. She and Freddy worked together at Patti's on the Pier. Well, I'm here to say that every once in a while, this creature of habit does return to haunt one and all. Kidding aside, this is a story of a lady who as a single mother grew to become a dining room manager who all learned to love. She was tough but she was always on the ball demanding excellence.

I, personally, cannot imagine a more difficult mountain to climb than that of being a single mom with 2 children to raise while juggling a strenuous work schedule. But she has, including guiding her son into becoming an eagle scout and into college. You're a special person, Renee. Never lose sight of the paths you've walked even when the incline ahead of you looks too steep to surmount. You're tough and we're all behind you just in case help is needed, which isn't very likely.

This is Ella Mae. What a jewel she was for Patti's. She could keep our kitchen together through the most hectic lunch rush imaginable. She was an unbelievably hard worker. She balanced raising a family which included taking care of her very ill mother and husband and still progressed at work. She grew to be one of our most capable managers. I'll never forget the tired looks on her face from all the juggling in her life. She won many awards while at Patti's which must have been about 10 or 12 years. But the one memory I cherish the most is when she got a job earning really big bucks with a construction company. If anyone deserved a better life, it was this lady.

Sometimes the Lord really does bring even greater fortune to us than we could ever imagine; whether it's an overabundance of love and happiness, professional fulfillment, pride in loved ones, or (at the risk of sounding superficial) financial fortune.

I think Ella Mae is happy today and that makes me very happy. She's shy and reserved so having her picture taken was not totally a comfortable position for her, but look at the bright, sparkling smile on her face. She is a doll and I hope her children know that she'll always be one of the greatest in the history of Patti's. They are lucky to have her as a mom and we are lucky to have had her for many years. Oh yeah, her soups were unsurpassable.

At left, you see the lovely and dynamic Jan Shipley-Cross receiving her Settlement Employee of the Year Award at one of our Christmas parties.

At left, John O'Bryan and Nathan Howard. Nathan started working at Patti's when he was about 15. He eventually married one of the servers he met here. He has gone on to bigger and better things, using his experiences and the work habits honed at the Settlement to carve out a successful life for himself. Nathan is soon to be remarried (I knew there was one marriage that didn't quite work out) and I wish him and his new bride total happiness and complete love for one another. John is now married and a father but other than knowing this, I can only hope he's happy and healthy. There are a great many people from Patti's past that we just lose track of.

Barbara McAbee started with Patti's years ago when Marian was our head decorator. When Marian decided to start Reflections at the Settlement, decorating was turned over to Barbara. She has grown both personally and professionally beyond every expectation in becoming a master artist with Patti's decorations. Barbara oversees the putting up and taking down of decorations over the course of an entire year, four seasons, holidays that occur every

month or two, and annual events that affect our lives such as the start of the school year. She's constantly planning and working out details for things like Valentine's Day, Mothers' Day, Paducah's Quilt Show, Halloween, Thanksgiving and Christmas. It never ends. She plans, buys and even merchandises all the creations you see, many of which are available for sale just in case you really like what she picked out and how she used it.

I'm most fond of the seasonal trees she keeps up year round. Many times I've heard people say they thought they'd go home and try something decorative they've seen at Patti's. Folks, when you come in the summer of 2000, check out her Miss Scarlet tree in Ashleigh's Boutique. I promise it will be a must see.

Keep growing girl and personally, I'm glad our little 'over the bridge' talk led your life in such a rewarding direction. Good luck and God bless.

Miss Mary is our version of Noah (only of Patti's ark). Since we started building The Settlement, children and families have always been a part of Patti's. We're in a dry county so it made sense to appeal to families. Besides, Mom loved kids and even became a daycare teacher after we all left home. We learned in 70% of American families, the children are the ones whose wishes are satisfied when choosing an outing and place to eat. We saw McDonald's and Burger King spending hundreds of thousands of dollars on playground equipment to attract children. We hired Mary to develop our animal park. We expanded old McBill's (Dad's) farm till it evolved into Miss Mary's farm. Mary originally took care of Dad's famous pigs. Now we have; possums, skunks, sheep, llamas, emu, deer, pigs, rabbits, geese, ducks, turkeys, peacocks and more. It's Mary's job, along with her husband Cliff, to care for all the animals.

Many of the animals are orphaned and brought to Patti's for raising. We received our raccoons when they were only a couple of days old. They were orphaned when their mother was killed by a car. She raised them by bringing them to work and then taking them home with her every day so they would have regular 2 hour feedings. Today, Mary walks the raccoons around The Settlement every day on her shoulder. They certainly have no fear of humans and probably wouldn't make it in the wild. Our deer are orphans also. We have the most fun in the spring when most babies are born. When we can, we set up like a petting park so kids visiting The Settlement can interact with the animals, both domesticated type and the wild ones like the deer and raccoons. Mary loves her animals so much, sometimes I wish I were an animal. They take such good care of them, sometimes I'm envious of them.

Thanks always Mary and Cliff. Be sure to bring children or grandchildren to our Settlement to experience our animal park.

Eat your heart out McDonald's!

Mary's husband, Cliff is 78 years young. He's our twice champion of Arielle's miniature golf classic and chief fence and barn raiser for Mary. A wonderful man and a great example of how vital the body can stay when the mind thinks it's still young.

This photo shows Mary with a three legged fawn that had been run over by a farm combine. Baby and her adopted mom were part of Patti's for several years until a strange deer disease killed them both within a couple of days of one another. I think it might be possible that one died of the disease and the other of a broken heart.

Mary's Easter wagon—it's out by the animals and
Mary decorates it from season to season.

Colonel, the llama, shown here expressing his contempt for the sheep eating
his food. We lost Colonel at age 12 which is the normal lifespan of llamas.

Two old but never forgotten Patti's employees are Steve Lloyd (left) and Barkley (Tooter) Gaines. Steve managed our kitchen for a while and then moved on to one of my favorite restaurants in the area, Jeremiah's, in Paducah. I'm just thankful he stuck with an independent and didn't migrate to a chain restaurant.

Tooter has been a server off and on for many years. He is now a realtor with Lake Realty here in Grand Rivers.

If there were ever a party nearby, you could be sure that Steve and Tooter were there with the man pictured here, Gary Fisher. Such a sweet soul. He was with us for years and I never saw him the least bit rattled or upset.

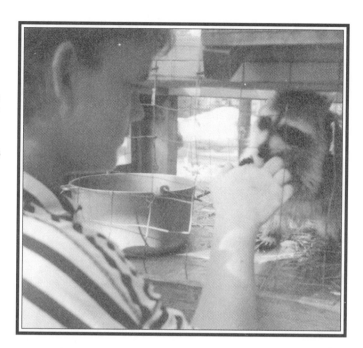

This picture is of Bandit, our first raccoon when he was young. He was my favorite raccoon because he loved to be held. We recently lost him at age 13. Bandit, I sure miss you!

Folks, one of the most difficult jobs is deciding what to wear for Halloween. You see, every year we have our employee costume contest.

Here is Jeff Cope, a resident pie person dressed like a Patti's waitress, looking as if to say, "More chocolate syrup on that boatsinker? You want more syrup? You'd better turn around and head on out to your tables or you'll get more chocolate syrup!"

Fun and laughter are two of the keys to keeping your sanity when it comes to restaurant work. One of the hardest jobs is getting all the soups, salads and desserts out on time (which is very quickly) to the right server.

Most of you who have frequented Patti's in the last four years will recognize this handsome gentleman. He's been a senior chart runner at Patti's for a while now. He's also about to graduate (spring of 2000) from Murray State University with a degree in horticulture. Eric Green has just taken a new position with our company. He is now our group reservation coordinator. He'll be the one arranging Christmas reservations and most all details for groups of 20 or more.

Congratulations on your promotion. We'll sure miss your expertise as a host.

Above: Holly, Deena Gail, Fowler
We find a great many fabulous servers from the student body at Murray State University.

At left: another Halloween girl, Mrs. Deena Gail Mitchell, mother of 2, wife and Patti's server for 12+ years. She's always impeccably dressed and this is no exception. Pictured as Lady Liberty, with photos of Mom, dad and Grandmother looking out the windows of her crown, this remains one of the best costumes of all time. I'm sorry I can't remember who the short little gnome next to her might be but Terry Vallelunga would be my guess. He was Mr. Bill's biscuit throwing trickster who grew 2 inches taller while working at Patti's. He always stated how vertically challenged he was. After college (he was engaged last time I talked with him) he was going to Atlanta or Florida to take an acting position. And this boy has real talent. Louie DePalma, look out!!!

Here, you see Kenny Dunning and Mitzi Prater. Mitzi is also a wife, mother of two and full-time server at Patti's. Since she and Deena work as one in the dining room and together can handle the load of three or more servers, I felt I should place them in the same area in the book. Folks, these two ladies epitomize all that Patti's stands for—gracious hospitality, home, family and professionalism.

These two, and many others, make up the players on Patti's stage. I really appreciate when they treat you well. And I also appreciate it when you, our customers, treat my staff well. After all, these aren't just any servers, these are Patti's servers; the cream of the crop. Let them get to know you while you are here.

Cappuccino

1½ cups powdered non-dairy cream	1½ cups sugar
1½ cups chocolate milk dry mix	½ teaspoons cinnamon
1 cup instant coffee granules	½ teaspoon nutmeg

Mix all ingredients together. Place 3 heaping teaspoons to coffee mugs; add hot water and stir until dissolved. Top with whipped cream.

Amie (who married
Mike), Scott and Travis

From the left: Cliff Grizzard,
Deana Southern, Mike Smith

Clockwise from bottom left: Vanessa
Capps, Andrea Davis, Nicole Jennings,
Doug Cole

178

Right: Freddie Jackson and our drama major, Terry Vallelunga

Above: Ericka Sisco, Holly Coleman, Teresa Sutton

Above: Madonna Boone, Kim Alexander, Angie Turner

Kim Alexander
and
Mary Anne Garland

Santa (played by Bear Darnell)
With a friend

Debbie Thaxton and Marge Jones

Think these three dressed alike on purpose or do they have the same taste in motor- cycles? Rachel Lujan, Gena Costello and Michelle Harper.

Gena is married to Mike Costello, one of Lisa's right hands in managing the dining rooms. He and Lisa and Chris Hatfield work hand in hand. Anyway, Gena and Mike have a darling daughter, Casey.

Remember John Lujan from earlier in the book? He was the server who married the gift shop manager Marla. They had a son, Cody. Rachel is John's sister. It's often a family affair around Patti's.

Miss Jean Wells, a working mother from our fair little city, is our chief dumpling maker and frier of chicken at the Iron Kettle. Here she is dressed for Hallow- een. I know there aren't many stories about the Kettle in this book because it's so new for us. But Jean, Rosa, Shorty, Phyllis and Jan are the backbone of the Kettle. See, the Kettle was an institution and it put Grand Rivers on the map long before Patti's came along. We've only been operating it for 2 years now.

But these 5 ladies have years of dedica- tion to The Kettle under their belts. Here's a special wish going out to Miss Sandy Jackson. You'll always be a part of our team. The spirit of the Lord be with you always.

Deannie and Darnell, you're doing a terrific job. You two keep on growing.....

Here you see Anna Mae Boone. She's now in her 90's and getting rather feeble, but she still has stories to tell of Grand Rivers in the teen's and 20's. She was one of the very first clerks in our gift shop back in the late 70's and early 80's. She is a fine example of the wonderful people who grew up in the tiny hamlet of Grand Rivers during this past century. She'll always be a part, a very fondly remembered part, of the history of Patti's.

Hostess Neeta Keeling co-wrote our first book about Patti's. It is still available in our gift shop.

Here is Deena Olson looking pretty in our first wagon wheel outfit when we didn't yet have air conditioning in our log cabins.

Jill, Etta and Mike (Gena's husband)
More Award Winners

Miss Norma Koontz along with
Marian and Etta have been in
charge of uniforms for years

Jamie Trombly, Emily Lamb
and Mike Costello

Miss Norma Koontz, again holding one of her many accomplishments. Notice she's standing where the new Patti's gift shop is being built. Also there are no buildings in the back forty, just llama pens.

Banana Nut Bread

2	sticks margarine	6	large bananas, best when very ripe
2	cups sugar	4	cups flour
4	egg yolks	4	egg whites
2	tablespoons water with 2 tablespoons soda, dissolved	1½	cup nuts

Mix margarine, sugar, egg yolks, soda with water and bananas. Beat well. Add flour and mix well. Beat egg whites and fold in. Bake at 350° for 1¼ hours. Makes two small pans or one large pan. Can be baked in a Bundt or tube pan.

A tip from Patti is to throw the brown bananas in the freezer, skin and all, when they become too ripe. They are easy to store this way and you'll always have them on hand when you are ready to bake banana bread.

Pictured here is Norvell—our head carpenter and also Lawana's father, Michael T.'s father-in-law and grandfather to Arielle, Anna and Adam (the next generation of Patti's owners)—

Lonnie with chainsaw in hand — he's always been a bit of a roughneck.

with his buddy and often partner in crime, Lonnie Evans. Lonnie has worked with us for many years, both as a part of our staff and as an independent contractor. He has been cook, kitchen manager at Patti's, kitchen manager at Patti's of Glasgow, gardener, carpenter, concrete contractor, tree surgeon, laborer, etc., etc., etc. He's husband to Scarlett and Dad to Derrick, Andrea, Rhea and Christian. I consider Lonnie the son I never had. He's the most Christian spirited man I've ever met. Jesus would approve of the love in Lonnie's heart. He loves unconditionally and non-judgmentally and is a very forgiving soul.

Lonnie, in his after dark dress — he's truly dressed to the nines — so many faces, look who ends up with the last laugh, ha, ha, ha...

Finally, let me introduce our neighbor, Jeanetta Newcomb. She's the mother of Mark (who owns and operates the Grand Rivers Antique Mall with his wife Sherry) and Troy (who has been our fire chief since he was in his teens) and wife to Jerry (who since retiring, is a tireless worker for the city of Grand Rivers). This is a very special family for the Tullars. The Newcomb family owned the motel before Mrs. Nash (who we bought the motel from). Miss Minnie Newcomb, Jerry's mom, lived next to the motel and restaurant for years till her recent departure from this life.

Jerry and Jeanetta live across the street from me and their back yard and side yard both adjoin our Settlement property. No better neighbors could a person hope for. Jerry keeps his house and yard in immaculate condition, as he does the rest of our city since he works in city maintenance. He keeps our little town very nearly spotless. He has been on the fire department since we moved here in 1977. He and Troy have answered fire calls at our properties at least 4 times over our 23 years. Needless to say, this is a family of wonderful people. I can only give deep, heartfelt thanks to the Newcombs for years of patience and understanding and support.

Sauces and Glazes, Seafood,
Vegetables, Cookies & Desserts
Through the Years
A Historical Tour of Patti's
1880's Settlement

This is the oldest photo I have of Mom and friends working the street
in front of the Grand Rivers Motel—notice cars behind them where the
round circular driveway went in front of the motel in 1975. We could
call these unidentified folks with mom our first Patti's family. Maybe
someday they'll recognize themselves and come forward. Remember
this motel had 6 units Mom rented for $7.50 to $11.50 a night.

Here you see the front of the old motel newly decked out with a western cedar porch which set the tone for all of our later additions. This was added to the old motel in 1976. The circular drive disappeared in about 1978 or 1979. This porch is still visible over the brick hallway at Patti's hostess area. Our first gift shop, which we built for Pat Moore was built onto left corner of the building in about 1979. Then she moved her Owl's Roost from the Canal Bait Shop into our building.

Here is a photo of me arriving from California with a few of our belongings in our Tonka truck as we called it. Michael Lee arrived a few months later in a big Ryder truck with the entire household. Notice the side of the building and its cinder block construction. The front of the building looked the same until Mom and Dad covered the cinder blocks with western cedar and put on the porch. Mom was a leader in the use of western cedar for external siding. It was soon as ubiquitous as lapboard. She always was a trendsetter—go, Mom, go.

Notice the concrete picnic tables and old Grand Rivers Motel sign. In the first years, we still were a motel with a single dining room restaurant seating 20 people. The steps you see leading to the street are in the same place as today, but today they're brick steps instead of wooden. Notice the slight slope to the street, no retaining wall.

Here you can see that the motel sign has come down and we are now a restaurant only. See Dad's Web-Core Kettle. He'd smoke the evening dinner special every Friday and Saturday in this kettle grill. The smell of smoking pork loin really drew people in for dinner later.

Roses—remember the family flower—line the circle drive of the old motel. Early on we grew them; actually all my life. At one time we numbered 400 bushes, back when Dad kept them. Also notice our first outdoor dining area, one of mother's yardsale finds. We painted this picnic set bright yellow and it sure was an attention getter.

Strawberry Topping

4 cups crushed strawberries	5½ cups sugar
1 box Sure-Jell	1 cup white Karo syrup

Pour Sure-Jell over berries and let set 20 minutes. Add sugar and Karo syrup. Mix well. Pour into small fruit jars or containers. Freeze.

*You can use this topping over ice cream,
or our favorite way, on homemade biscuits.*

Recipe submitted by Donna Keeling

Notice the addition on the left side of the photograph. This was the Owl's Roost
Gift Shop (added 1980) which is now our Trophy Room. Notice our first sign
which designated us "Patti's 1880's Restaurant." At this point, we were no longer
Hamburger Patti's Ice Cream Parlor. Look at those fancy customer cars. Hopefully, we've all prospered over the years.

Today, this same sign still exists.

In about 1981 or 1982, we converted the Owl's Roost to a dining room, enclosed the entire front yard to provide our garden room dining room, hostess station and first gift shop (Yesterday Once More Antiques and Gifts). Notice at this point, we have pushed the property back some and built up the hill with a retaining wall to provide more parking out front.

Ham Glazes

½ cup of orange marmalade,
   peach preserves, currant jelly
   or grape jelly

¼ cup nuts ground

Mix together and cover hot baked ham, return to oven, 15 to 20 minutes at 350°.

1 tablespoon dry or prepared
  mustard

¼ cup fruit juice, cider, or tomato
  juice
White or brown sugar

Mix mustard with liquid of your choice. Brush the surface of the baked ham with this mixture. Sprinkle with either white or brown sugar. Return ham to oven for 15 to 20 minutes in a 350° oven

1 cup white or brown sugar

¼ teaspoon each ground cloves,
  allspice, nutmeg, mace, and
  cinnamon

Mix together and cover hot ham, return to 350° oven and bake 15 to 20 minutes.

Here, the retaining wall is draped with old barge ropes salvaged from the beaches. The rose gardens are developing and the ivy, which now covers the retaining wall, is starting to take hold. Not much has changed with the entrance and front of the building since 1981 or 1982.

Apple Custard Sauce

⅓ cup flour
1   cup sugar
1   teaspoon ground cinnamon
¼   teaspoon ground nutmeg

2   cups apple juice or water
⅓   cup white vinegar
⅓   cup butter or margarine

Combine flour, sugar, and spices in 1-quart saucepan. Stir in juice, vinegar, and butter gradually. Cook over moderate heat, stirring constantly until thickened. Remove from heat and serve warm over apple dumplings, cobbler, apple cake, etc.

Makes about 2½ cups

Various Glazes

Tangy Lemon Glaze

Place 1 cup sifted powdered sugar in a small bowl. Add 2 teaspoons lemon juice and ⅛ teaspoon grated lemon rind. Gradually add about 4 teaspoons hot milk, blending well, until mixture is thin enough to spread.

Makes about ⅓ cup

Rum-Flavored Glaze

Place 1 cup powdered sugar in a small bowl. Gradually add ½ teaspoon rum extract and about 1 tablespoon hot milk, blending well. Mixture should be thin enough to spread.

Makes about ⅓ cup

Orange Sugar Glaze

Place 1 cup powdered sugar in a small bowl. Gradually add about 1 tablespoon hot orange juice, blending well. Mixture should be thin enough to spread.

Bonbon Glaze

Place 1 cup sifted powdered in a small bowl. Gradually add about 1 tablespoon hot water, blending well. Mixture should be thin enough to spread. Add ⅛ teaspoon almond extract and a drop or two of food coloring, to tint to a light shade.

Makes about ⅓ cup

Chocolate Glaze

Melt 1 square unsweetened chocolate with 1 tablespoon butter, over low heat. Remove from heat and add ¾ cup unsifted powdered sugar and a dash of salt. Blend in about 2 tablespoons hot milk, a small amount at a time, until mixture is thin enough to spread. While still warm spread over cake.

Makes about ½ cup

This picture is looking at the front of the building, a view of the Owl's Roost door. Notice that our front entrance and Yesterday's gift shop aren't built yet. In the photo below, the gift shop exists.

1981—next to Patti's was my brother's mobile home and next to that was my grandmother Tullar's cottage. Today, this space is occupied by our gift shop, Yesterday Once More. If you think of our bricked front hallway, it ends in front of Patti's men's room which is at this end of the building. The new section, the carpeted gift shop area was built out to the right of the building and displaced the trailer.

Basic Brown Sauce

2 tablespoons butter
3 tablespoons flour
1 cup beef stock

½ teaspoon salt
Dash of pepper

Melt the butter, add the flour and cook the two together until thoroughly browned. Stir frequently, but not necessarily constantly, to prevent scorching, over a very low flame. Add the seasonings and the stock gradually, bring to boiling point and cook five minutes. If desired, or if more convenient, bouillon cubes and water may be substituted for the meat stock. Also a slice of onion may be cooked with butter and flour if desired, and will make the sauce somewhat more savory.

*This brown sauce is now ready to serve as the base
for raisin, piquante, Madeira sauce, etc.*

Chunky Artichoke Salsa

1 jar (6.5-ounce) marinated
   artichoke hearts
¼ cup pitted ripe olives, chopped
2 tablespoons red onion, chopped
3 medium plum tomatoes,
   coarsely chopped

1 garlic clove, pressed
2 tablespoons fresh basil leaves,
   snipped
Salt and ground black pepper, to
   taste
Lettuce leaves

Drain marinade from artichokes. Mix all ingredients together.

Serves 6

This was our first office and it came into existence when Patsy and Gail were part of Patti's—this is where the ladies' rest room at Patti's is now. Our offices are now located over our kitchen area. Notice the couch—it's where I usually took a nap to get through the day. Originally, we opened at 6:00 am for breakfast.

Here's a photo of Jewell's Bait Shop (it has all the signs out front) which burned down in 1998 while Jewell was cooking sausages for breakfast—also a commercial was shot here for Chrysler's first mini-van using Jewell's as a backdrop. Billy Ray Cyrus also did a video shoot on Harleys in front of Jewell's. Today, this is a parking lot adjacent to Patti's.

Curry Sauce

1   cup brown sauce (recipe
     included in this book)
1   tablespoon onion, minced

1   teaspoon curry powder
1   teaspoon tomato paste

Slightly brown onions in butter, add to brown sauce. Blend with curry powder, (first moistened with a little brown sauce.) Add tomato paste to mixture.

Suitable for meat, fowl, vegetables, fish or eggs. All
sauces to be served on hot foods should be sizzling hot.

Hollandaise Sauce

½   cup butter
3   egg yolks
2   tablespoons lemon juice

¼   teaspoon salt
¼   teaspoon freshly cracked white
     pepper

Melt butter, which should be very hot when you are ready for it. Put egg yolks and 3 tablespoons cold water in a small non-aluminum pan. Whisk them together over high heat, raising and lowering the pan to control heat; the pan must not get too hot. Whisk continuously until mixture starts to mound and is the consistency of heavy cream. Remove from heat and whisk in ¼ cup of the hot melted butter 1 tablespoon at a time. Return pan to heat and add remaining butter in a thin stream, whisking continuously. Whisk about 5 minutes or until the mixture is thick and creamy. Remove the pan from the heat if it starts to get too hot, but don't stop whisking. Add lemon juice, salt, and pepper. Hold sauce in a pan of warm water until serving time.

Makes ¾ to 1 cup

Next to Jewell's was the Shorty Owens property which included this little house. A detached garage next to it and beyond that, a large empty lot filled with a life's accumulation of personal treasures. Today, this house is our shipping and receiving department and (pictured below) the garage with the cedar log siding I put on it is now a part of C & A Christmas Exchange. You can still see the front of this building when you go in the front door. This was our first log cabin and inspired the development of our Settlement.

Pictured here is a panoramic view of our streetscape, circa 1981

This is what our present gift shop looked like in 1981.

This is how this area looks today after the final 1996 addition.

Jezebel Sauce

1 (12-ounce) jar pineapple
  preserves
1 (5-ounce) jar Coleman's mustard
1 (12-ounce) jar apple jelly

1 (5-ounce) jar horseradish
Salt to taste
Freshly ground black pepper to
  taste

Combine all ingredients with an electric mixer. Keeps indefinitely in refrigerator. Serve over ham.

Makes 3 cups

Madeira Sauce

2 cups brown sauce (recipe
  included in this book)

1½ tablespoons Madeira wine

Reduce brown sauce to ½ its original volume. Add Madeira wine, if too thick, thin with brown sauce.

Suitable for roast dark meats or smoked meats.
All sauces to be served on hot foods should be sizzling hot.

Rum Sauce

4 tablespoons butter or
  margarine
1 (14-ounce) can condensed milk
1½ cups sugar, or to taste

¼ cup dark rum or 1 teaspoon
  rum extract
⅛ teaspoon salt
¼ cup finely chopped pecans (may
  omit)

In a small saucepan, melt butter and stir in remaining ingredients.

Cook and stir over low heat until mixture is warm and flavorful, about 5 minutes. Serve over gingerbread, bread pudding or meats.

Makes about 1½ cups

Piquante Sauce

2 tablespoons white wine
1 tablespoon vinegar
1 teaspoon minced shallots
1 cup brown sauce (recipe included in this book)

1 tablespoon sour pickles, finely chopped
1 teaspoon minced parsley
1 teaspoon minced chives
Pinch of tarragon

Combine white wine, vinegar, and minced shallots. Reduce to ½ volume, add to brown sauce. Just before serving, stir in chopped pickles, parsley, chives, and tarragon.

Suitable for pork, leftover meats and smoked meats.
All sauces to be served on hot foods should be sizzling hot.

This is the back of our property in the middle 1980's. Three feet behind our building begins Mr. Bill Ridlen's property. The old station wagon was his. You can see the back side of Michael T's mobile home.

This is another view of the Ridlen property with my house (The Thomas Lawson/Tullar House) in the background, circa 1985.

Raisin Sauce

1 teaspoon sugar	1 cup brown sauce (recipe included in this book)
1 teaspoon vinegar	¼ cup seedless raisins

Carmelize sugar with vinegar. Combine with brown sauce and just before serving , stir in raisins plumped in hot water or stock, then thoroughly drain.

Suitable for roast ham, pork, or game.
All sauces to be served on hot foods should be sizzling hot.

Bill Ridlen's mobile home, his old bait store, and notice the old station wagon behind Patti's first dining room, the one with Indian Joe in the bathroom. This property became ours in 1985 except that the trailer and lot didn't become ours until 1999. The vacant building in the center became Wilman's Antiques and David Williams and Fred Eddleman operated this business for several years.

Mr. Ridlen's mobile home as it sat until 1999

Scalloped Scallops

1½ pound scallops	1 teaspoon grated onion
¼ cup butter	1 teaspoon finely minced parsley
4 cups soft bread crumbs	1 teaspoon finely minced chives
1¼ teaspoon salt	1 tablespoon lemon juice

If using large scallops, quarter or slice them. Melt the butter, add all remaining ingredients, and toss together thoroughly. Arrange in a generously buttered baking dish. Alternate layers of scallops and the crumb mixture, having crumbs for the top layer. Bake in a hot 400° oven about 20 minutes, or until delicately browned.

Serves 6

Crab Omelet

½ pound crabmeat	1 teaspoon parsley, cut fine
4 eggs, beaten	1 teaspoon salt
1 large onion, cut fine and fried in little butter	¼ teaspoon pepper

Mix in order given and fry when ready to serve.

Crabmeat Bisque

1 can of green pea soup	1 can of tomato soup

Heat well, stirring constantly.

Add:

1 can of crabmeat	1 cup cream

Heat thoroughly, add ¾ cup sherry. Serve very hot!

Very good with lobster or shrimp.

207

In 1988, after closing Patti's on the Pier and Patti's of Glasgow, we built a huge addition to our kitchen at Patti's 1880's Restaurant. We added the upstairs as our new offices. Also in 1989-1990, we began construction of the Mr. Bill's addition to Patti's, notice that there are no trees or gardens. See that our house is clearly visible from Commerce Ave. before Mr. Bill's is built, this photo shows the Settlement before any gardens, cabins, streams or walks are constructed.

1990 view of rear of Mr. Bill's and newly constructed fountain.
Walkways and gardens are just being started.

Shrimp and Cheese Casserole

1½ pounds cooked shrimp
4 slices bread, remove crust and butter both sides
3 eggs, well beaten

1½ cup milk
1 teaspoon salt
Dash of paprika
2 cups grated cheese (not sharp cheese)

Cut bread in 1-inch squares, and line the bottom of a 2-quart baking dish. Add layer of shrimp and layer of cheese. Continue in layers, ending with cheese layer. Sprinkle seasonings over mixture. Add milk to beaten eggs. Pour over shrimp mixture. Bake 45 to 60 minutes, with casserole sitting in pan of hot water, in 325° oven.

This photo is of Mr. Bill's under construction. An interior shot, you can see Marcus' folk art painting of old, new and future Grand Rivers in the center of the photo.

Here you see the sidewalks are being poured that connect Patti's to Mr. Bill's. They were our first sidewalks. We'd only had gravel walks before this; what an improvement. Notice that the raised gardens on the left hadn't been built yet. We didn't yet own the property across from Patti's on the main street so we decided to concentrate on improving the land behind the restaurant. This is why the main gift shop entrance is oriented to the rear of the property and the gardens that were springing up.

Shrimp Creole

4	tablespoons oil	½	cup green onions, chopped
4	tablespoons flour	1	medium bell pepper, chopped
1	medium onion, chopped	1	clove garlic, minced
1	stalk celery, chopped	1	can tomato sauce
1½	pounds peeled shrimp	2	cups hot water

Use oil and flour to make a roux. Add onions and celery to the roux, cook until onions are clear. Add tomato sauce and 3 cups of hot water. Simmer for 20 to 30 minutes. Add shrimp, green onions, bell pepper and garlic. Season and salt to taste, simmer for 20 minutes more. Serve over cooked rice

This recipe was submitted by Lisa Galusha who gives credit for the recipe to Jill Choate, a former employee.

Shrimp Dip Mold

¾ cup boiling water
1 small package lemon gelatin
1 tablespoon lemon juice
3 tablespoons horseradish

1 package unflavored gelatin,
  dissolved in ¼ cup cold water
1 (12-ounce) bottle chili sauce
2 (4-ounce) cans shrimp, drained

Dissolve lemon gelatin in boiling water, cool slightly. Add remaining ingredients and pour into well oiled 3½ cup mold. Chill until set. Serve with club crackers.

Shrimp Gumbo

5 pieces of bacon
2 cups sliced okra
1 tablespoon flour
1 onion, chopped

1 can tomatoes
1 pound fresh or canned shrimp
Salt and pepper

Fry bacon and take out of skillet. Fry okra in bacon grease after rolling in flour. When half done add onion and cook. Add tomato and cook. Add shrimp and let it heat through—if fresh a little longer. Lastly, crumble bacon in mixture. Serve over rice.

Swiss Crabmeat

½ cup butter
½ bunch chopped green onions
½ bunch chopped parsley (no
  stems)
2 tablespoons flour
1 (16 ounce) can evaporated milk
½ pound Swiss cheese, grated

Worcestershire sauce to taste
Cayenne pepper to taste
Salt to taste
1 pound crabmeat, drained
¼ cup sherry
Pastry shells

Melt butter and sauté onions and parsley. Add flour and cook over low heat for 5 minutes. Add milk slowly, stirring with wire whisk. Add cheese and cook until melted

Add seasonings, then crabmeat and sherry. Cook until hot. Serve in pastry shells.

Serves 8

This photo shows the Delsa Rose room being built on the back of the old motel building. The open doorway is the door you walk through to enter the Delsa Rose room. It's named in honor of Grandmother Delsa Tullar and our family flower, the rose. Notice, that the gift shop addition (the area to the left in the photo) is built later.

This is a view from the same open doorway looking out to the back garden area, looking at the garden construction. Notice the back of Mr. Bill's on the left side of the picture and Mr. Ridlen's mobile home in the far background.

Adam's Potato Wedges

8-10 red potatoes, peeled

¼ cup canola oil

Salt and pepper to taste

Garlic powder to taste

Once potatoes have been peeled, slice them into wedges and place in a bowl of cold water to soak for 15 minutes. Drain on a towel. Put wedges back into a bowl and top with canola oil, salt, pepper, and garlic powder. Stir potatoes with seasonings. Coat a baking sheet with nonstick spray and spread potatoes out on sheet. Bake in a preheated 400° oven for 15 minutes or until wedges are slightly brown or done with a fork.

"Adam likes to use ketchup when eating his potato wedges."

Adam, 16 months old

Here, you see the rear of the Delsa Rose room almost completed. Stage one of the garden development is nearing completion.

Cliff, a cousin of Lawana's and her dad, Norvell,
puts finishing touches on the Delsa Rose room.

Baked Vegetable Medley

1½ cups fresh corn (about 3 ears)
¾ cup peeled, chopped tomato
⅓ cup cornmeal
2 cups (8 ounces) shredded
   cheddar cheese
1 medium onion, chopped

1 medium-size green pepper,
   chopped
2 eggs, beaten
¾ cup milk
½ teaspoon salt
Dash of pepper

Combine first 6 ingredients: let stand 30 minutes. Spoon into a lightly greased
12x8x2-inch baking dish. Combine remaining ingredients, pour over
vegetables. Bake at 325° for 35 to 40 minutes or until set.

Serves 8 to 10

Broccoli Puffs

2 (10-ounce) packages frozen
  broccoli
1 (10¾-ounce) can cream of
  mushroom soup
½ cup American cheese, grated
¼ cup milk
½ cup mayonnaise

2 tablespoons cooking sherry
1 egg, beaten
½ teaspoon salt
Dash of pepper
1 tablespoon margarine, melted
¼ cup fine, dry bread crumbs
¼ cup sliced almonds

Thaw broccoli and drain well. Place broccoli in 10x6x2-inch baking dish.
Thoroughly blend together soup, cheese, milk, mayonnaise, sherry, egg, salt
and pepper. Pour over broccoli. Combine margarine with bread crumbs and
sprinkle over broccoli-soup mixture. Sprinkle sliced almonds over crumb
mixture. Bake in 350° oven for 45 minutes, or until crumbs and almonds are
brown.

8 servings

Cheese-Stuffed Zucchini

4 medium zucchini
½ cup (or more) Italian seasoned
  breadcrumbs
⅓ cup freshly grated Parmesan
  cheese
1 egg, beaten to blend
½ teaspoon garlic powder

½ teaspoon dried thyme, crumbled
½ teaspoon dried oregano, crumbled
½ teaspoon freshly ground pepper
Salt
¼ cup shredded cheddar cheese
¼ cup shredded Monterey Jack
  cheese

Bring large saucepan of water to boil. Add zucchini and cook until just tender,
about 15 minutes. Remove from water using slotted spoon. Cool slightly.
Preheat oven to 350°. Combine ½ cup breadcrumbs, Parmesan, egg, garlic
powder, thyme, oregano, pepper and salt in large bowl. Slice zucchini in half
lengthwise and scoop out center pulp. Coarsely chop pulp and drain. Add to
breadcrumb mixture and blend well. (If mixture is too wet, add more breadcrumbs.)

Spoon mixture into zucchini halves. Sprinkle with cheddar and Monterey
Jack. Transfer to baking sheet. Bake until heated through and cheese bubbles,
15 minutes.

4 servings

In 1992, we began the new addition to Patti's gift shop and new entrance to Patti's. This is where Michael T's mobile home and Grandmother's cottage stood, before her wall heater caught fire one December. She managed to escape with her life, thank God, but that was all. Our excellent volunteer fire department was able to prevent any damage to the mobile home and to Patti's.

Here, you see the progression of the gift shop construction. After the house burned down and Michael T. bought a house in town. Colonel, the llama, resided in the area behind the photographer along with a burro and Shetland pony.

Corn Fritters

1 cup all-purpose flour	1 cup fresh cut corn
1 teaspoon baking powder	⅔ cup milk
1 teaspoon sugar	1 teaspoon butter, melted
½ teaspoon salt	Vegetable oil
2 eggs, beaten	Powdered sugar

Combine flour, baking powder, sugar, and salt; mix well. Combine eggs, corn, milk, and butter: mix well and stir in dry ingredients. Drop mixture by tablespoonfuls into vegetable oil heated to 375°. Cook until golden brown, turning once. Drain on paper towels. Sprinkle with powdered sugar. Serve hot.

Makes about 2½ dozen

This photo shows the gift shop nearing completion.

May 1992—gardens were only completed along new sidewalks. Here you can see the newly completed gift shop addition in the background.

Fried Green Tomatoes

6   medium-size fresh green
    tomatoes, cut into ¼-inch
    slices
1½ cups buttermilk
1   cup cornmeal
½   cup unbleached flour
1   tablespoon salt (needed for
    green tomatoes)

Freshly ground pepper
1½ teaspoons cayenne pepper
2   teaspoons dried thyme
¼   cup peanut oil
¼   cup vegetable oil

Soak the tomato slices in buttermilk. Mix the cornmeal, flour, and spices together. Dredge the tomato slices in the cornmeal mixture. Heat oil in a large skillet. Sauté tomatoes over medium heat for about 2 minutes per side or until golden. Drain on absorbent towels and serve immediately.

This is the area behind Patti's and Mr. Bill's showing the second stage of garden development. Notice the gravel walkways. Laying the walkways out with gravel enables us to see if they serve our traffic flow adequately before pouring concrete sidewalks. At this point, Michael T. and I are more of a team in building The Settlement. We began to talk more together about how things should go. Usually I was the designer and he and Norvell figured out how to build it.

Fried Potato Cakes

4   cups shredded potatoes, fresh
    or frozen
2   eggs, lightly beaten
½   cup chopped onion
⅓   cup all-purpose flour

3   tablespoons minced fresh
    parsley
1   teaspoon salt
1   teaspoon pepper

Rinse potatoes in cold water, drain thoroughly. Mix potatoes, eggs, onion, flour, parsley, salt, and pepper. Pour batter by ⅓ cupfuls onto greased hot griddle or skillet.

Fry on each side until golden brown.

Makes about 10 pancakes

Honey Glazed Carrots

8   medium carrots, scraped
¾   cup water
2   teaspoons sugar
¼   cup honey

2   tablespoons orange juice
2   tablespoons butter or margarine
½   teaspoon salt

Cut carrots in half crosswise, then slice halves lengthwise into quarters. Combine carrots, water, and sugar in a saucepan. Cover and cook 5 to 8 minutes or until crisp-tender. Drain carrots, reserving ¼ cup of cooking liquid. Set aside. Combine ¼ cup carrot liquid and next 4 ingredients in a saucepan. Bring to a boil and cook 5 minutes. Add carrots and reduce heat. Simmer 2 to 3 minutes.

Serves 4 to 6

Here, the gardens are in the middle of major development. This is stage two for the gardens. Notice Grandpa Norvell with his most recognizable straw hat trying to figure out what I've come up with for him to do next. I suspect that in his head, he's working out the details of our first gazebo.

Hoppin' John

8	ounces dried black-eyed peas	1	cup rice, uncooked
4	ounces bacon	2	cups water
3	tablespoons olive oil	⅓	cup red bell pepper, minced
1½	onions, chopped	½	cup Parmesan cheese
1	tablespoon salt, freshly ground pepper	¼	cup scallions, minced
1	teaspoon butter	⅓	cup green pepper, minced

Soak peas overnight covered with water in a large bowl. Drain. Fry the bacon crisp and set aside to drain. Reserve 2 tablespoons of the drippings and place them with olive oil in large skillet. Cook onions over medium heat for about 8 minutes or until translucent (not brown). Place peas in a large Dutch oven with enough water to cover. Add the onion mixture, getting all the flavoring oils. Add salt and pepper. Bring to a boil and them reduce heat to a slow simmer for 40 to 45 minutes. Add more water if needed as cooking. Peas when done should be tender and most of the water absorbed. Boil 2 cups of water and any remaining liquid from the black-eyed peas as part of the water. Add the butter and 1 cup rice. Cook 18 to 20 minutes until tender. Combine the peas and rice, heat through, and serve. Garnish with crumbled bacon, minced pepper, scallions, and Parmesan cheese.

Serves 6 to 8

Onion Pie

3	tablespoons butter	2	cups half and half cream
2	cups sliced onions	1	teaspoon nutmeg
½	cup grated Swiss cheese	½	teaspoon salt
4	eggs	1	9-inch unbaked pie shell

Preheat oven to 400°. Sauté onions in butter, stirring until they are limp. Sprinkle onions in pie shell; cover with grated cheese. Beat eggs; stir in cream and seasonings. Strain into pie shell. Bake on lowest rack of oven for 15 minutes. Reduce oven temperature to 325°. Bake for another 30 minutes or until a knife inserted 1 inch from edge comes out clean. Top should be lightly browned.

Serves 6

Here you see the stone creek being created. The handsome Lonnie Evans of Evans Lawn Care and my adopted son—ha,ha. Lonnie's great. He started at Patti's when he was about 16 as a cook. He moved up to kitchen manager and then moved his family with me to open Patti's of Glasgow when his twin daughters, Andrea and Rhea were 11 days old. Then he returned home to start his landscaping business and to this date, cuts all the lawns and helps build all major landscaping jobs. Here he was helping me build our first water system.

Notice the animal pens on the left and though you can't see it, Patti's is on the right. Dead center is the colossal water fountain next to the bridge. The second phase of garden development was on its way.

Orange Beets

1 can frozen orange juice
1 can water, (use orange juice can measure)
¾ cup cider vinegar
1 ¼ cups brown sugar

2 tablespoons cornstarch
1 tablespoon butter
1 #2½ can of beets, whole small type

Moisten the cornstarch and smooth to a paste using ½ of the water. Mix all the other ingredients except the butter and beets. Bring to a boil and add the cornstarch. Stir to prevent lumping and cook until clear and thickened, about 8 minutes

Add the butter, then the beets. Heat well and serve.

Scalloped Eggplant

1 large eggplant, peeled
1 cup crushed crackers
1 cup shredded cheese
1½ cups milk
4 eggs, beaten
1 teaspoon salt

½ teaspoon pepper
½ cup melted margarine or butter
½ cup shredded cheese
½ cup cracker crumbs
1½ tablespoons margarine or butter

Heat oven to 325°. Cook eggplant in boiling water until soft; drain. Combine the eggplant, 1 cup crushed crackers, 1 cup shredded cheese, milk, eggs, salt, pepper and ½ cup melted margarine; mix well. Mix the ½ cup cheese, ½ cup cracker crumbs and 1½ tablespoons margarine in a bowl until crumbly. Spread over the top of the eggplant mixture. Bake for 25 to 30 minutes.

Serves 6

Here I am in the fountain on opening day. The water was supposed to cascade evenly over the top of this huge stone fountain and splash over all the stonework to the creek down below. Well, let me say it was a disaster from the get go. Each one of those stones had been put there by hand and some sloped inward and some sloped outward. Hindsight's 20-20 and we never anticipated the consequences. The water ran back behind the rocks rather than over the front of them. It drained out of the bottom center of the fountain and hardly a trickle could be seen on the outside of the fountain. From there it drained to the street in front of Patti's. Needless to say, it had to be torn down and I suffered a major architectural and financial blunder. The water wheel cabin/ garden shop now occupies this site.

May, 1992——we were looking mighty fine.

Here you see Colonel's new home and more new sidewalks Lonnie has developed with flat sandstone imbedded in concrete. I think they're beautiful, but they're quite hard to lay. Notice there is no development in the back beyond this point. This is a view of where the Wagon Wheel log cabin will soon sit. This was the first site out back to be developed in our new Patti's 1880's Settlement.

Skillet Cabbage

½	medium cabbage	1-2	tomatoes
1	medium onion	1	tablespoon bacon drippings
1	bell pepper	1	teaspoon salt
3	stalks celery	¼	teaspoon pepper

Chop the vegetables fairly fine. Melt the bacon drippings in a skillet; toss in chopped vegetables. Season with salt and pepper. Mix well, cover and cook over moderate heat. Stir occasionally, cook for 5 to 8 minutes or until cabbage is tender-crisp.

Serves 4 to 6

Spinach and Feta Pie

½ pound phyllo dough
1 pound spinach
2 tablespoons olive oil
1 onion, finely chopped
1 tablespoon chopped fresh dill

3 eggs, beaten
4 ounces feta cheese
Salt and pepper
4 tablespoons butter, melted

Heat oven to 375°. Cut phyllo leaves to fit your baking pan and cover with damp cloth. Prepare the spinach. Heat oil in skillet and fry onion for 5 minutes until soft. Add spinach and stir for 5 minutes over medium heat; increase heat to take up moisture. Allow to cool, then mix in dill, eggs, cheese, salt and pepper. Brush melted butter in baking pan. Brush 8 phyllo leaves with butter. Lay in bottom of dish. Spread on filling and cover with remaining leaves. Brush each one with melted butter and scoring the top into diamond shapes. Sprinkle with water and bake for 40 minutes until crisp and golden. Let stand for 10 minutes. Cut into wedges and serve.

Here, The Colonel's new home. See our house in the background. The Settlement is coming along. Also there's a fun thing to note here. It's a joke here at Patti's—every time the Colonel moves, so goes another stage in the development of Patti's. This was move number two. First he lived in the area that is now our main gift shop, then he was moved to here.

Spinach Ring

4 (10-ounce) packages frozen
   chopped spinach, thawed and
   drained
1 cup medium white sauce
2 tablespoons prepared mustard

2 tablespoons Roquefort or blue
   cheese, crumbled
1 teaspoon grated onion
Salt and pepper to taste
1 cup bread crumbs
3 eggs, separated

Combine first 6 ingredients. Stir in bread crumbs and beaten egg yolks. Whip egg whites until stiff but not dry. Fold into spinach mixture. Pour into a greased 2-quart ring mold. Set in a pan of hot water. Bake covered at 350° for 25 to 30 minutes. Turn out on a platter and garnish with parsley.

Serves 8 to 10

Here, we're showing off Lonnie's beautiful walkways.

Stuffed Acorn Squash

Halve the squash and remove the seed and pulp. Cover the bottom of a baking dish with boiling water. Bake squash, cut side down, in a hot oven, 400°, for about 30 minutes or until tender. Sprinkle squash with salt and pepper. Stuff the hollowed centers with mashed potatoes, sausage or dressing. Return to oven and brown.

Stuffed Tomatoes

6 large tomatoes, very ripe	1 tablespoon fresh, parsley, chopped
Salt	2 teaspoons honey
1 cup black-eyed peas, cooked	Freshly ground black pepper
1 cup baby lima beans, cooked	3 tablespoons fresh mint, chopped
⅓ cup olive oil	
1 tablespoon balsamic vinegar	

Slice off the stem end of the tomatoes leaving ⅔ of tomato. Hollow out the tomatoes, reserving all pulp. Salt the tomato "cups" then turn upside down to drain. Coarsely chop all pulp and combine in a large bowl with the remaining ingredients. Fill tomatoes with the bean mixture. Garnish with mint and serve.

Serves 6

Yellow Squash Puppies

2 cups cooked and mashed yellow squash	¾ cup self-rising cornmeal
1 small onion, chopped fine	¼ cup self-rising flour
1 small bell pepper, chopped fine	½ cup buttermilk
	1 egg

Cook as "Hushpuppies."

Notice that we finally have water running down the creek. Also notice that every tree and plant you see in the gardens was brought in and planted. The gardens have come a long way over the years.

Mr. Bill's Barnyard directional sign

Here, we start the development of the lower fountain system.

Homemade Pepper Relish

12 red hot peppers
12 green hot peppers
12 medium-sized white onions

2 cups sugar
2 cups vinegar

Grind the hot peppers in a meat grinder and put in a strainer. Grind onions in a meat grinder and mix with sugar and vinegar. Run hot water over the hot peppers for several minutes (the longer you run the water over the peppers, the milder your relish will be). Put peppers in the onion mixture and cook over medium heat for approximately 20 minutes.

Makes 4 pints

This recipe submitted by Anita Williamson

Tempura Vegetables

2	medium zucchini	¼	teaspoon pepper
2	medium-sized yellow squash	½	cup water
1	medium onion	1	large egg, lightly beaten
¾	cup cornstarch		Corn oil
½	cup self-rising cornmeal	½	teaspoon salt

Cut vegetables into ¼-inch thick slices. Separate onion slices into rings. Combine cornstarch, cornmeal, and pepper, then stir in ½ cup water and egg until smooth. Dip vegetables into batter. Pour oil to a depth of ½-inch into a heavy skillet; heat to 375°. Fry vegetables, in batches, 4 minutes or until golden. Drain on paper towels; sprinkle with salt.

4 servings

This recipe submitted by Janice Rogers. She notes that this is the original family recipe but now she omits the salt and pepper and substitutes Patti's Pork Chop Seasoning.

This is the lower fountain system finished.

Here's a picture of the gardens today. Note that Colonel the Llama has moved again (move number three) and the Wagon Wheel log cabin now resides where he used to.

Here, Norvell and company start the new gazebo's development—
notice the side of my house just to the right of the chimney.

Chocolate, Coconut, and Pistachio Macaroons

3 large egg whites, at room
  temperature
⅛ teaspoon salt
1 cup sugar
6 1-ounce squares of unsweetened
  chocolate, melted

1 cup sweetened flaked coconut
1 scant cup shelled pistachios,
  finely chopped
¼ cup semisweet chocolate chips,
  melted

Heat oven to 350°. Lightly grease 2 baking sheets. Beat whites and salt with electric mixer, until frothy. Gradually add sugar, beating until very light and fluffy, about 5 minutes. Very gently fold chocolate, coconut and ¾ cup pistachios into beaten whites. Drop by rounded measuring teaspoons, 1 inch apart, onto greased baking sheets. Bake macaroons 10 to 12 minutes or until just firm. Turn off oven; leave in oven with door slightly ajar 30 minutes for interior of cookies to crisp. Transfer to wire racks. Drizzle melted chocolate chips over tops of macaroons and sprinkle with remaining nuts. Cool completely. Store in airtight container.

"Livingstone" is quarried here in Livingston County and is used in the fountains, streams, sidewalks and here is used to build a planter. Mr. Holsapple is the gentleman who furnishes us with all of the stone. If you see a pile anywhere around it means something is about to be built.

Date Balls

1 egg, beaten	2¼ cup Rice Krispies
1 cup sugar	1 cup chopped pecans
1 package chopped dates	1 can shredded coconut
1 teaspoon vanilla	

Combine egg, sugar, and dates in saucepan and heat just until sugar is melted. Remove from heat. Add vanilla, Rice Krispies and pecans. Mix well. Shape small balls and roll in coconut.

Store in container with tight fitting lid.

Flowers, beautiful flowers—our family has always taken pride in our yards. I guess it goes back to the days of family Sundays when we all worked in the yard together, then had more family time grilling out and eating. Usually, the Reese family or the Leggett family were there for dinner. These were my best memories of us as a family. Today, Sunday seems to be family day at Patti's. Everyone's been to church, out boating, fishing or camping. Whatever they've been doing, it is their family time and I get the greatest pleasure watching everyone walk around and enjoy what our family's yard and house are like today—just a little larger than in years past—but not really any different than it was on our Sundays when I was growing up.

Today, we have six full time gardening and maintenance crew members; Linda Dunbar, Judy Boren, Abby Carter, Vince Halligan, Justin Walker and Jim Brogoto (our maintenance man and Joe fix everything man). It's a huge expense, especially the watering but it's all free to you to enjoy. It's our family's gift to your families and friends for all the years you've been dining with us. It's our gift from God's blessings and we, in turn, work to create that special heavenly place here on earth where you can slow down, feel God, His love and marvel in his glorious works, the beauty of nature. Let Him touch you. If you slow down enough, allow yourself to sit quietly for a while in our tiny meditation chapel. It's non-denominational and intended for everyone, no matter what his or her beliefs. It and it's gardens are imbued with a peaceful spirit that, for a few minutes or hours, may just lift you up and carry you or it may hold and comfort you if that's what you need from The Spirit.

Easy Chocolate Chip Cookies

1 box yellow cake mix	1 egg
¼ cup brown sugar (packed)	¾ cup oil
½ cup nuts	1 cup chocolate chips

Mix first 3 ingredients. Blend egg and oil then add to cake mix mixture. Add chocolate chips. Drop by teaspoon onto ungreased cookie sheet. Bake at 350° for 8 to 10 minutes.

Mocha Chocolate Chip Cookies

3 cups semisweet chocolate chips	½ teaspoon salt
½ cup butter (1 stick)	4 egg, room temperature
4 ounces unsweetened chocolate	1½ cups sugar
½ cup all-purpose flour	1½ tablespoon instant coffee powder
½ teaspoon baking powder	2 teaspoons vanilla

Melt 1½ cups chocolate chips, butter and unsweetened chocolate in top of double boiler set over hot but not boiling water. Stir until smooth. Remove from over water. Preheat oven to 350°. Line baking sheets with parchment or waxed paper. Combine flour, baking powder and salt. Beat eggs, sugar, coffee powder and vanilla in large bowl of electric mixer at high speed 2 minutes. Stir in chocolate mixture, then flour. Add remaining 1½ cups chocolate chips. Drop batter onto prepared sheets by teaspoons, spacing evenly. Bake until cookies are crackled and shiny outside but still soft inside, about 8 minutes; do not overbake. Cool completely before removing from sheets. Store in airtight container.

Makes about 7 dozen

Rolled Honey Wafers

2 cups sifted flour	1 cup shortening
¼ teaspoon nutmeg	1 cup sugar
½ teaspoon cinnamon	2 cups honey
1 cup shredded almonds	2 eggs, well beaten

Mix and sift flour and spices; stir in almonds. Cream shortening until soft; beat in sugar, then honey and eggs; stir in flour mixture. Drop small portions from teaspoon on greased cookie sheet, about 2 inches apart. Bake in slow oven (300°) about 12 minutes or until delicately browned. Cool 1 minute, then remove with spatula and roll, top-side out, around handle of wooden spoon, or roll cone-shaped, or fit into a tea cup. Keep in covered container to keep crisp.

Makes approximately 80 wafers

We should be glorifying all God's living things, as we should be giving a certain amount of glory to each other unconditionally, because being made in God's image and being his supreme earthly beings, we should have reverence for the value inherent in each other. Now, look at all these diverse flowers. They have different heights, colors, shapes and fragrances. Yet, each is beautiful in its own way. We should view our fellow humans in the same loving way in spite of and even because of our differences.

Find peace in our gardens. The Peace of the Lord
be with you—always.

Here we go, the development of Patti's 1880's Settlement, circa 1992. After we experienced some reasonable success in our gift shop, I realized that there was no way Patti's would survive unless we answered the threat posed by the retail giants surrounding us; Kentucky Oaks Mall and Eddyville Outlet Mall. With the coming of all the chain restaurants who had such advantages as better location, cheaper raw material purchasing through volume discounts, liquor and huge marketing budgets, we had to do something. They could subsidize their food operations through higher profit margins thanks to liquor and lower purchasing costs. And for quite a long while, it seemed like another chain restaurant was opening in our region every week. Same amount of people eating out, but a lot more seats to fill. We had to find a way to draw people in from outside our region or else we would fail. In 1991, we saw our business decline after years of steady growth.

Cracker Barrel caught my attention. They were making it without alcohol. How? I noticed that 40% of their floor space was devoted to retail. So, I decide that retail was where we were growing next.

I realized that Disneyland had become a huge success as a family entertainment center and destination in its own right. Look at Disney World. Walt bought huge amounts of land out in the middle of nowhere and the people came and came and came. Look at Orlando, Florida today. So I recognized Disneyland is built with Adventureland, Tomorrowland, Fantasyland, etc. Combining and adapting Cracker Barrel's retail and Disney's entertainment/attraction concepts could help turn our little town into the destination it had to be in order to compete regionally.

Patti's 1880's Settlement was created on paper with the help of my longtime artist friend, Roger Morris. He takes my ideas and puts them on paper for Norvell and Mike to build. So, we started planning and building. Here is a $15,000 log cabin from Possum Trot, KY. It was, at one time, the Griggstown general store and post office. As a dog trot cabin, the store was on one side and the postmaster/ storekeeper lived in the room on the other side. It became our first log cabin retail store.

Here, the cabin is being moved into place—where it has become our Wagon Wheel gift shop. Folks, Thomas Lawson came to Grand Rivers in about 1889 and took pictures of it before he started building the little Victorian village. There were 12 log cabins in our town when he arrived. Today, we have six back in the general area. Therefore, we created Grand Rivers—post Thomas Lawson. We, like Disney, will have several different areas someday. But ours will be before Thomas Lawson (prior to 1889), post Thomas Lawson (Victorian village after 1890), and today.

Southern Pecan Cookies

1 package yellow cake mix
1 packages butter pecan instant
     pudding mix

1 cup chopped pecans
1 egg
1 cup vegetable oil

Combine ingredients; beat well. Roll into 1-inch balls. Bake on lightly greased cookie sheets in 350° oven for 8 to 10 minutes.

Top of Stove Cookies

½ cup milk
2 cups sugar
½ cup butter
2 rounded tablespoons peanut
     butter

2 tablespoons cocoa
1 teaspoon vanilla
3 cups oats, uncooked

Combine milk, sugar, butter and peanut butter in pan. Boil hard 1 minute. Remove from heat. Add remaining ingredients, mixing well. Drop by spoonfuls on waxed paper. Let dry.

Fudge Pie

4 cups sugar
1 cup cocoa
6 eggs
1 tablespoon flour

1 tablespoon vanilla
2 sticks butter (melted)
1 large can evaporated milk
1 deep dish pie crust

Melt butter and add sugar and mix well. Add cocoa. Add eggs, one at a time and mix after each one. Add flour and vanilla. Add milk and mix well. Bake at 350° for 45 minutes or until pie is set.

Lisa Galusha submitted this recipe but admitted that it was her mother's.

With the Wagon Wheel cabin in place (upper left corner), two more cabins were brought in for "Reflections, A Mirror of Memories." This gift shop is shown here under construction. You see folks, we could get hardly any retail stores to survive in our town because our season was so short and Patti's really was the only business to have very many people. So I decided if we built the retail around Patti's where the people were, we'd eventually be able to grow the town so to speak. It's been a very tough process—the malls and Walmart are very hard to compete against. Most little towns in America are drying up because of this and we are trying to build our little town up.

Needless to say, bankers thought I was crazy and said it couldn't be done. But we're doing better, little-by-little, thanks to you folks who come and shop our shops, walk our walks, and tell your friends so we can spend our small profits on more development. Some day we hope to truly be a destination spot and if we work harder and smarter and provide a better experience, we will be able to compete against the malls. Today, in the year 2000, we have one more threat to compete against; on-line shopping. Y'all keep your fingers crossed.

Apple and Nut Pie Dough

1¼ cups flour
10 tablespoons sugar
Salt

1 egg
9 tablespoons butter, cut into pieces

Filling

1 pound dessert apples, peeled, cored and sliced
¼ cup ground hazelnuts
1 teaspoon cinnamon
Juice of 1 lemon

3 tablespoons apricot brandy (optional)
½ cup apricot jam
½ cup chopped nuts

Sift flour and sugar (saving 2 tablespoons of sugar for filling) and a pinch of salt, into a mixing bowl, make a well in the center and add the egg. Mix in the butter pieces, and work the ingredients together to make a soft smooth dough. Place the dough in the refrigerator for 30 minutes. Grease an 8-inch pie dish. Roll out the pastry and place in pie dish. Preheat oven to 425°. Layer apple and hazelnuts in the pie shell. Sprinkle with cinnamon, reserved sugar, lemon juice and apricot brandy. Put apricot jam in a saucepan and heat until melted. Pour over filling. Sprinkle with chopped nuts. Bake until the pie is golden and the fruit is soft. Serve warm or cold.

Michael Lee and I found this old corn crib out in a field in southern Illinois. The old farmer sold it to us for $1,500. Michael T., then went out with his crew, numbered the logs, tore them down and brought them back to the Settlement.

Here, Michael T., brother Craig (home on vacation), Norvell (under the straw hat), and Dad are busy working on the Wagon Wheel. The cabin on the left was once a jail in Graves County. The cabin on the right is the corn crib we found in Illinois. They were joined together to form one cabin shop in the Settlement.

Here is a better picture of the corn crib and old jail being resurrected. At first, we didn't air condition the stores because we wanted the Settlement to be more authentic. Then, we decided it wasn't fair to our employees and to our customers to have to endure such uncomfortable conditions. It turned into a living historic village—and the air conditioning made it livable.

Another thing we discovered is that you folks don't really care for small stores. People poked their noses in and then turned around and left. So, we've had to join some stores together to make them larger. Eventually, the chimney on the old post office we moved from Possum Trot came down and these two buildings, three separate cabins originally, were joined together.

Apple Pecan Crisp

4 cups tart apples, sliced and
   sprinkled with lemon juice
¾ cup brown sugar, packed
½ cup sifted plain flour
½ cup rolled oats

¾ teaspoon cinnamon
¾ teaspoon nutmeg
½ cup butter, softened
½ cup pecans, chopped

Butter 8-inch square pan. Spread apples on bottom. Blend remaining ingredients until crumbly. Spread over apples. Bake at 350° until apples are tender and top is golden brown, about 30 to 45 minutes. Serve with whipped cream or ice cream.

Serves 6

Apricot Nectar Cake

1 package plain yellow cake mix
¾ cup cooking oil
1 small package lemon gelatin

2 teaspoons lemon juice
¾ cup apricot nectar
4 eggs, separated

In mixing bowl combine cake mix, oil, gelatin, lemon juice, apricot nectar and egg yolks (one at a time, beating well after each addition). In another bowl, beat whites until stiff. With spatula, gently fold egg whites into cake batter. Pour mixture into well greased and floured tube pan. Bake at 325° for 45 minutes to 1 hour or until cake tests done.

Icing
½ cup orange juice

2 cups powdered sugar

Mix together ingredients for icing, making a glaze. Spoon over cake when cool.

Michael T. and Mom with her miniature pinchers she raised for extra cash. Here, they're talking with a friend in front of the completed Wagon Wheel gift shop. I'm sure glad Mom switched from raising German shepherds to raising min-pins.

Here is a photo of "Reflections," our gift shop managed by Marian Bauguss, being moved onto the property. It was always exciting for me to see a sight like this. It meant life was good. The town was growing and even prospering.

Banana Split Cake

5 bananas	1 large can crushed pineapple, drained
2 cups graham crackers	1 large tub frozen whipped topping
3 sticks butter, softened	1 cup chopped pecans
2 eggs	1 small bottle maraschino cherries
2 cups powdered sugar	

Mix 2 cups crushed graham cracker crumbs with 1 stick butter. Press in pan. Beat for 15 minutes, 2 sticks butter, 2 eggs, 2 cups powdered sugar. Pour over crumbs and slice bananas over mixture. Top with pineapple. Cover with whipped topping. Top with pecans and cherries. Refrigerate for 2 hours before serving.

This recipe submitted by Teresa Sutton.

Berries 'N Cream Cake

1 (15-ounce can) Eagle Brand sweetened condensed milk	1 pint fresh strawberries, quartered
⅓ cup lemon juice	1 cup heavy cream
1 tablespoon grated lemon rind	8 ladyfingers

Combine first 3 ingredients; fold in berries. Whip ½ cup of the cream until stiff. Fold into mixture. Split ladyfingers; line 9x5x3-inch loaf pan, bottom and sides. Pour berry mixture into pan, keeping ladyfingers in place. Refrigerate until firm. Run spatula around inside of cake pan to remove cake. Invert pan on plate. Whip remaining cream stiff and ice cake. Decorate with berries.

Buttermilk Icing

3 cups sugar	2 tablespoons corn syrup
1 cup butter or margarine	1 teaspoon baking soda
1 cup buttermilk	1 cup finely chopped nuts

In a large heavy saucepan over medium heat, heat first 5 ingredients. Bring to a boil and cook to 238°. Beat with mixer about 7 minutes on high speed; add nuts and frost cake.

Here you can see the cabin that will be Reflections turning onto the Settlement grounds off of the main street. This is just north of C & A Christmas Exchange.

There were two of these cabins which were a part of another family's dream to create a heritage village on Highway 641 in Marshall County. It was heart-breaking when that dream didn't survive. We bought these two of their cabins and brought them to Grand Rivers. I hope that family's dreams are somewhat kept alive by our incorporating them into our Settlement, though I'm sure it's difficult for them to see. We left the cabins apart as a breezeway sort of like an old dog trot cabin. Also, this way, our historic home a half block away was clearly visible. But eventually we had to enclose that area to make the shop larger for your shopping enjoyment. The two cabins were soon one.

Cantaloupe Sorbet

3 tablespoons sugar
3 tablespoons water
1 large cantaloupe, halved,
    seeded, peeled and cut into
    chunks

2 tablespoons fresh lime or lemon
   juice

Cook sugar and water in heavy small saucepan over low heat until sugar dissolves, swirling pan occasionally. Increase heat and bring to boil. Cool syrup to room temperature. Puree cantaloupe in processor or blender. Transfer to bowl. Stir in syrup and lime juice. Pour into ice cream maker and process according to manufacturer's instructions.

Caramel Icing

3 cups sugar
1 stick butter

1 cup milk
½ teaspoon vanilla

Combine 2½ cups sugar, the butter, and milk in a 3 or 4 quart pot, begin cooking. Brown ½ cup of sugar in skillet and add to the syrup already cooking. Cook to 238° (soft ball stage). Remove from heat; cool. Add vanilla and heat to consistency for spreading. If icing becomes too stiff, a little cream may be added to thin.

Chess Bars

1 package yellow cake mix
1 egg

1 stick margarine, melted

Mix in large bowl of mixer until crumbly and pat into 13x9x2-inch pan.

1 (8-ounce) package cream cheese
3 eggs

1 teaspoon vanilla extract
1 box powdered sugar

Mix well in large bowl of mixer and pour over above mixture. Bake 350° for 45 minutes, or until set. Let cool and cut into bars and sift with additional powdered sugar.

Before being placed on a foundation and before porches were added.

New porches are being added here—my family loves porches. It's a part of Southern heritage we really fell in love with.

Chewy Date Nut Bars

1	package yellow cake mix	2	eggs
¾	cup packed brown sugar	2	cups chopped dates
¾	cup butter or margarine, melted	2	cups chopped walnuts

Combine cake mix and brown sugar. Add butter and eggs; beat on medium speed for 2 minutes. Combine dates and walnuts; stir into batter (the batter will be stiff). Spread into a greased 13x9x2-inch baking pan. Bake at 350° for 35 to 45 minutes or until edges are golden brown. Cool on a wire rack for 10 minutes. Run a knife around sides of pan to loosen; cool completely before cutting. Cut into bars or squares.

Makes 3 dozen

Chocolate Coconut Pie

2	cups milk	3	eggs
¾	cup sugar	¼	cup butter, melted
2	tablespoons cocoa	1	teaspoon vanilla
½	cup biscuit mix	1	cup shredded coconut

Grease 9-inch glass pie plate. In a blender, combine all ingredients except coconut. Blend on low for 1 or 2 minutes. Pour into prepared pie plate. Allow to set for a few minutes, then top with coconut. Bake on middle shelf of preheated 350° oven for 35 minutes or until knife inserted in center of pie comes out clean. Good hot or cold.

Coconut Balls

Scoop out balls of vanilla ice cream. Roll in freshly grated coconut or fresh frozen. Freeze firm again; in a shallow dish keeping each ball separate until serving time.

Serve garnished with Crème de Menthe, or chocolate sauce and finely chopped roasted nuts. Easy dessert and very attractive!

Coconut Cream Pie

⅓ cup of sugar

¼ cup of cornstarch

¼ teaspoon salt

1 (8-ounce) can cream of coconut (¾ cup)

3 beaten egg yolks

2 tablespoons butter or margarine

1 cup flake coconut

2 teaspoons vanilla

1 (9-inch) baked pastry shell

3 egg whites

½ teaspoon vanilla

¼ teaspoon cream of tartar

⅓ cup sugar

2 tablespoons flake coconut

Filling: combine first ⅓ cup sugar, cornstarch and salt. Stir in milk and cream of coconut. Cook and stir over medium heat until thickened and bubbly. Cook and stir 2 minutes more. Gradually stir about 1 cup of the hot mixture into the beaten egg yolks, stirring constantly. Return all of the mixture to saucepan. Cook and stir until full bubbly again. Cook 2 minutes. Remove from heat. Stir in margarine or butter until melted. Stir in the 1 cup coconut and 2 teaspoons vanilla. Pour into pastry shell. Meringue: Let egg whites stand at room temperature for 30 minutes. Beat egg whites, ½ teaspoon vanilla and cream of tartar on medium speed until soft peaks form. Evenly spread meringue over hot filling, seal to pastry edge. Sprinkle with the 2 tablespoons coconut. Bake 15 minutes in a 350° oven. Cool for 1 hour on a wire rack. To serve cold , cover and chill 3 to 6 hours.

Serves 8

Here, we have a saw mill set up to manufacture our own logs to replace unusable ones rotted by weather or not long enough. Also, we can make our own cedar shake roof shingles. We did that for several cabins but insurance rates have sky-rocketed due to the wood shingles. We're using red tin roofs on all the buildings and it's becoming one of the trademarks for Grand Rivers.

Cranberry Sorbet

1 pound cranberries	2 cups sugar
3 cups boiling water	⅛ teaspoon salt
1 tablespoon gelatin	1¼ cups orange juice
½ cup cold water	1 tablespoon lemon juice

Cook berries in boiling water until soft. Soak gelatin in cold water 5 minutes. Combine berry puree with sugar, salt and juices in a heavy sauce pan. Bring to a boil. Stir in gelatin, blending until thoroughly dissolved. Cool. Freeze until almost firm. Beat until light and fluffy. Freeze until firm.

Deep Dish Cranberry Apple Pie

¼ cup raisins	1 teaspoon cornstarch
¼ cup dark rum	½ teaspoon cinnamon
1 cup cranberries (thawed if frozen) chopped coarse	Pie crust recipe of your choice, rolled to 12 inches
1 cup sugar	1 egg, beat with 1 tablespoon water (egg wash)
8 Golden Delicious apples, peeled, sliced ⅓-inch thick and tossed with 1 tablespoon fresh lemon juice	1 tablespoon unsalted butter

In a small bowl let the raisins marinate in rum, heated, for 15 minutes. In a small heavy stainless steel or enameled saucepan cook the cranberries, with ⅓ cup of the sugar over high heat, stirring until the sugar is melted. In a large bowl combine the apple, the cranberries, the remaining ⅔ cup sugar. Add the raisin mixture, the cornstarch, and the cinnamon. Toss the mixture until it is combined well. Transfer it to a 2 quart 10-inch round ceramic or glass baking dish. Roll out your pie crust dough into a 12-inch round. Cover the top of your baking dish and trim off excess dough. Moisten the edge of the dough and underside edge of the dough. Press the dough onto the rim of the dish, crimp. Cut a 4-inch X in the center of dough and turn back the 4 corners. Moisten them and press the tips onto the dough lightly, exposing the filling. Brush the dough with the egg wash, dot the exposed filling with the butter. Bake in a 425°, preheated oven, for 20 minutes. Reduce heat to 350° and bake for 40 minutes more. Serve from the baking dish with whipped cream or ice cream.

Notice when standing on the new porches of Reflections cabins, the empty lot where Ashleigh's will be built and the Ridlen trailer is in the background. The pile of wood blocks are what the shake shingles start out as.

Look ladies, it's a fixer upper—no, it's Tara—no, it's actually the Mitchell family home in Burna, as talked about in the story. This home was probably our greatest treasure. The Mitchell family gave us the house for four free dinners at Patti's. They were going to burn it down. The home was located about 40 miles from Patti's and could not be moved whole due to road obstructions. So, we had to dismantle and rebuild it log by log.

The Mitchell house in its original setting. At The Settlement, it was rebuilt as Ashleigh's Boutique. Ashleigh's Boutique is named after my niece, Ashleigh Tullar, who is my brother Craig's daughter.

Diet Strawberry Pie

1 box diet strawberry gelatin	3 tablespoons cornstarch
6 whole graham crackers, crumbled	1½ cups water
Artificial sweetener to taste	3 tablespoons diet margarine
4 cups strawberries	

Mix graham cracker crumbs, sweetener and margarine and press in pie pan. Bake in 350° oven for 10 to 15 minutes and cool. In saucepan, cook gelatin, cornstarch, and water until thick. Cool and mix with fruit and pour in shell. Refrigerate until set.

This recipe was submitted by Mary Anne Garland

Easy Chocolate-Cherry Chews

1   package family size brownie mix   1½ cup chopped candied cherries
1½ cup flaked coconut

Prepare brownie mix according to package directions. Add cherries and coconut. Pour into greased 12x8-inch pan. Bake at 350° for 30 to 35 minutes (or 325° if using glass pan). Frost if desired. Cool and cut into squares.

Makes 15 bars

Maraschino cherries may be substituted for candied cherries.

When siding is removed, you can see the logs underneath.

Easy Orange Cake

2 cups whole wheat pastry flour
1 cup sugar
2 teaspoons baking powder
¼ teaspoon salt
½ cup butter or margarine, softened

1 tablespoon grated orange rind (2 or 3 oranges)
¾ cup orange juice, preferably fresh
2 eggs

Put flour, sugar, baking powder, salt, butter, orange rind, juice and eggs in large bowl of electric mixer. Stir, then beat at medium speed for 3 minutes, scraping bowl occasionally. (Batter will be very stiff). Turn into greased and lightly floured 8-inch square pan. Bake at 350° for 35 minutes or until pick inserted near center comes clean. Spread at once with glaze. Cut in squares while slightly warm or cool.

Orange Glaze

Mix until smooth, 1 cup powdered sugar and 3 teaspoons orange juice or enough to make a moderately thick glaze. Drizzle over cake.

Egg Custard Pie

1 10-inch pie shell, prebaked 15 minutes at 350°
5 eggs, beaten
1½ cups granulated sugar

2 cups warm milk
Pinch of cornstarch
Grated nutmeg

Line pie shell with waxed paper and fill with dried beans or peas (weight down crust). Bake at 350° for 15 minutes. Remove paper and beans. Combine eggs, sugar, milk and cornstarch. Pour into pie shell. Sprinkle with nutmeg. Bake at 350° for 45 minutes to one hour or until custard is set.

Serves 6 to 8

The whole back part of the house was rotten and unusable. The one thing we weren't able to save was the old stone chimney. We really weren't skilled enough to reconstruct it. The stones were used in the golf course development.

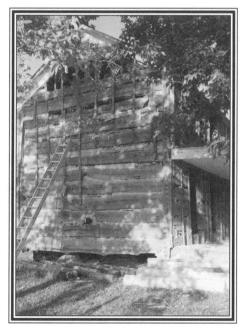

Here, the boys are taking the siding off and you can see the end logs.

Hurry Up Cracker Jacks

1   stick margarine   ½   teaspoon baking soda
1   cup brown sugar, packed

Mix well and boil 5 to 6 minutes, stirring constantly. Take off stove and add ½ teaspoon soda, stirring well. Pour over one bag of popped microwave popcorn in a large bowl and mix well with buttered spoon. Pour onto oiled cookie sheet and spread out to cool.

Submitted by Janice Rogers

As you can see, the interior was pretty rough.

Here, you see the fireplace end of the house after reconstruction. Notice the small window in both the previous picture and this picture.

Mississippi Mud Cake

4 eggs	⅓ cup cocoa
2 cups sugar	1 tablespoon vanilla
1½ cups flour	1 cup coconut
2 sticks margarine	1 cup pecans

Beat eggs and sugar, set aside. Combine remaining ingredients, then mix into egg and sugar mixture. Bake in 13x9-inch greased pan for 30 minutes at 350°. After taking from oven, immediately spread with 1 jar of marshmallow crème.

Frosting

1 box confectioners' sugar	1 teaspoon vanilla
⅓ cup cocoa	1 stick margarine

Combine all ingredients together and frost cake. Sprinkle with nuts.

This recipe submitted by Lisa Galusha who gives credit for it to her mother-in-law, Christine Galusha.

This is the spot where the Mitchell home is soon to be rebuilt as Ashleigh's Boutique. The wooded area in the background will soon be Arielle's Woodland Miniature Golf.

Mother's Rice Pudding

1½	cup sugar	½	cup raisins
3	tablespoons flour	1½	teaspoons vanilla
2½	cup milk	2½	cups cooked rice
2	eggs, beaten	Nutmeg	

In a large saucepan, stir flour into sugar. Beat in eggs, milk, and raisins, and cook, stirring constantly, until thickened. Stir in vanilla and rice. Pour into greased baking dish, sprinkle with nutmeg. Bake at 350° for 30 to 40 minutes.

Mounds and Chocolate Bars

2 packages flaked coconut	1 bar paraffin
1 can sweetened condensed milk	2 packages semisweet chocolate chips

Combine coconut and milk. Press into a buttered 9x13-inch pan. Refrigerate. Cut in small squares. In double boiler, combine paraffin and chocolate chips and heat until melted, stirring constantly. Remove from heat and dip mound squares into chocolate until completely covered. Place on waxed paper to set.

This recipe was submitted by Mary Anne Garland.

Here begins the reconstruction of the Mitchell cabin.

Old-Fashioned Jam Cake

4	eggs	1	small jar raspberry preserves
½	pound butter (melted)	1	teaspoon ground allspice
1	teaspoon salt	1	teaspoon ground cloves
1½	cups milk or grape juice- preferably juice	2	tablespoons ground cinnamon
		1½	cups nuts (pecans)
1	large jar seedless blackberry jam	3	cups flour

Bake in a Bundt pan for 30 minutes at 350°. Turn down the oven to 300° and continue baking until done. Cake is usually done in an hour.

Recipe and story submitted by Marjorie Rea

Here, Ashleigh's is on the way to completion. Again I used my living historic adaptation in the recreation of this log cabin. I was in Atlanta at the market with Mom, Miss Ellen, Marla, Karen and Laurie when we saw the beautiful stained glass window and door that now grace the rear of Ashleigh's. $10,000 later they are built into the new addition. The large, clear windows on either side of the stained glass I found in a salvage store and turned them upside down on top of each other. I didn't hammer a nail. Michael T. and Norvell did most of that. Remember, I'm not the carpenter. I'm the designer and creative type. Together, we three make a great team. Norvell is a very innovative and resourceful person. Michael T. was nearly killed by a falling log while rebuilding this structure. You might say he has a special relationship with this building.

Ashleigh's, nearly completed with porch rails and roofing yet to go. Notice, however, that the open sign is up and business has begun. I hope the Mitchell family and their family's heritage has been done proud. Always, thank-you for helping bring this treasure to us.

Desserts Mud Pie Crust

1 stick softened margarine	1 cup finely chopped pecans
1 cup flour	

Mix and press into a 9x13-inch pan. Bake at 350° for about 20 minutes or until light golden brown.

1st Filling

1 cup powdered sugar	½ of a 13-ounce tub of whipped topping
8 ounces softened cream cheese	

Mix until smooth. Spread over cool crust.

2nd Filling

1 small package of vanilla instant pudding	1 small package of chocolate instant pudding
	2⅔ cups milk

Beat until thick. Spread over first filling. Then top with remaining whipped topping.

This can be made with a plain graham cracker crumb crust as well.

This recipe was submitted by Jan Quarles and Charlotte Myers.

Pete's Pound Cake

½ pound butter
3 cups sugar
6 large eggs

1 cup whipping cream
3 cups sifted cake flour
1 teaspoon vanilla

Cream butter and sugar. Add eggs and cream alternately with flour, beating well after each egg. Add vanilla. Pour into well-greased and floured tube pan. Place in cold oven and turn oven to 325°. Bake for 45 minutes to 1 hour.

Serves 12 to 16

Here begins the ground work for Arielle's Woodland Miniature Golf Clubhouse— Arielle is Michael T.'s and Lawana's oldest child.

Prune Cake

1   cup prunes

Cook prunes in water to cover for 30 minutes. Refrigerate at least 24 hours in juices. Drain and chop prunes.

2 cups sugar	1 teaspoon salt
1 cup vegetable oil	1 teaspoon cinnamon
3 eggs, beaten	½ teaspoon ground cloves
1 cup buttermilk	1 teaspoon nutmeg
2 cups flour	1 teaspoon vanilla
1 teaspoon baking soda	1 cup chopped pecans

Mix sugar and oil together, add eggs and mix well. Blend in buttermilk and prunes. Sift together flour, soda, salt and spices. Add to prune mixture. Add vanilla and pecans. Bake in greased and floured tube or Bundt pan. Bake at 350° for 55 to 60 minutes.

This log cabin was purchased for $1,500 and moved here in one piece. It needed complete re-chinking and of course, true to form of making this a living historic cabin, we added the addition to the back so it would be functional for us. Here I am, contemplating what should go where. Everything is usually in my head and is developed as we go along, with everybody's input. That's one thing I've learned in life, I don't always have to know everything. I believe the more minds you put together to create a thought, the better.

The golf course under construction. This has been our most expensive project to date.

Pumpkin Chiffon Pie

3   egg yolks
1   cup granulated sugar
1¼ cups cooked pumpkin
½   cup milk
½   teaspoon each: salt, ginger,
      nutmeg and cinnamon

2   teaspoons gelatin dissolved in ¼
      cup water
3   egg whites
1   pre-baked 9-inch pie shell

Beat egg yolks with ½ cup sugar. Add pumpkin, milk and seasonings. Cook in top of double boiler, stirring constantly until thick. Add gelatin and stir until dissolved. Cool. Then into pumpkin mixture, fold egg whites that have been stiffly beaten with remaining ½ cup sugar. Pour into baked pie shell. Chill. Garnish with whipped cream.

6 large servings

Here, the golf course is open for play.

Quick Chocolate Chip Frosting

1 cup semi-sweet chocolate chips
   (6-ounce package)
¾ cup butter or margarine

1½ cups sifted powdered sugar
2 teaspoons vanilla

Microwave chocolate in small bowl for 1 minute. Stir and microwave ½ to 1 minute longer.

Stir until smooth. Beat butter and sugar until creamy. Blend in vanilla and chocolate until smooth. Frost cooled cake.

Raspberry Cake

3 eggs
1 package white cake mix
1 package raspberry gelatin

¾ cup oil
1 cup frozen raspberries (drain well)

Beat eggs, add cake mix, then dry gelatin and oil. Beat for 4 minutes. Fold in raspberries. Pour into 2, 8- or 9-inch greased and floured round cake pans. Bake at 350° for 30 minutes (or until firm in middle). Ice with a Butter Cream or Cream Cheese Icing.

Arielle's clubhouse and course, finished. I think it is a beautiful adaptation to the woods into which it is placed. It is very expensive to keep up, however, and it's really not a money maker. It's just a great thing for the families. You know, good, quality entertainment that's drug free and closely monitored.

Sour Cream Cake

1   package Duncan Hines Butter
    Recipe Golden Cake mix
3   large eggs
1   cup dairy sour cream

⅓   cup oil
¼   cup water
2   tablespoons sugar

Mix all and beat at medium speed with electric mixer. Pour into a greased 10-inch tube pan. Bake at 350° for 45 to 55 minutes or until knife inserted in center of cake comes out clean. No icing is needed for this cake.

This recipe submitted by Janice Rogers

The next to last building in this stage of phase one, which was started in 1991. This was a playhouse from Marshall County that we bought for $1,200 and had Mr. Ruggles move to the Settlement. Mr. Ruggles moved all of our structures except the old Graves County jail, the corn crib and the Mitchell home. I'd like to have a little fun here and see if you can figure out where it ended up. Now you can see what you can do with something like this too! The roof has been cut off so it can be moved.

Need some help?

Sauerkraut Chocolate Cake

⅔ cup butter or margarine softened
1½ cup sugar
1 cup water
3 eggs
1 teaspoon vanilla
½ cups cocoa (unsweetened)
2¼ cups sifted flour (all-purpose)

1 teaspoon soda
1 teaspoon baking powder
¼ teaspoon salt
⅔ cups chopped, drained and rinsed sauerkraut
Cocoa Whipped Cream

Cream butter with sugar until light and fluffy. Beat in eggs with butter and sugar. Add flour sifted with dry ingredients and water. Stir in sauerkraut. Prepare 2 9-inch cake pans. Bake at 350° for 30 minutes until done.

Cocoa Whipped Cream
1 cup heavy cream
½ teaspoons vanilla in bowl
2 tablespoons cocoa

2 tablespoons sugar
Dash of salt

Mix well and chill for one hour.

Strawberry Coffee Cake

3 ounces cream cheese
¼ cup butter
2 cups biscuit mix

⅓ cup milk
½ cup strawberry jam

Cut cream cheese and butter into biscuit mix until crumbly. Blend in milk. Turn out onto a slightly floured surface. Knead 8 to 10 times. On waxed paper, roll dough to a 12x8-inch rectangle. Turn onto a greased baking sheet; remove waxed paper. Spread strawberry jam down center of dough. Make 2½ inch cuts at 1-inch intervals on long sides. Fold strips over filling. Bake at 425° for 12 to 15 minutes

Drizzle coffee cake with icing (Powdered sugar and hot water mixed, not too thin.)

Makes about 8 servings

Sugar-Glazed Strawberries

2 cups sugar
1 cup water

2 pints extra-large strawberries
with stems

Line baking sheet with aluminum foil; butter foil. Heat sugar and water in heavy 1-quart saucepan over low heat, swirling pan occasionally, until sugar dissolves. Increase heat to medium-high and boil until syrup registers 300° (hard-crack stage) on candy thermometer. Reduce heat to very low. Working quickly, skewer 1 berry and dip into syrup, leaving leaves and stems exposed. Lift from syrup with swirling motion to remove excess. Slide onto prepared sheet, using fork or spatula. Repeat with remaining berries. Let glaze harden before serving. (Can be prepared 1 hour ahead.)

Makes about 8 servings

Finally, an outdoor exhibition center and wedding chapel. One day I saw a small child run behind a car parked in the upper parking lot which had a lot of foot traffic because of the shops all around it. While backing up, the car almost hit the child. I knew then that we had to do something. So the pavilion which is the center of any small town, was developed to be the center of ours. In 1999 we had 43 weddings and 2 nights of Karaoke, a Christmas pageant and 2 flower shows. It's all made from our lumber which was sawn on site by Norvell and it was completely designed by him. I think it's beautiful. Michael T. assisted as always and is responsible for all the landscaping you see around the gazebo. It has been the jewel in our ring of cabins and the culmination of old Grand Rivers reborn.

Walnut Torte

1 cup graham cracker crumbs	4 eggs, separated
1 teaspoon baking powder	½ cup sugar
1 cup ground walnuts	½ pint cream, whipped

Crush and roll the graham crackers into crumbs. Mix these crumbs with the baking powder and nuts. Beat the egg yolks until thick and lemon-colored, beat in the sugar. Gradually stir in the crumb and nut mixture. Fold in gently but thoroughly the stiffly beaten egg whites. Turn into 2 greased and floured 8-inch layer cake pans. Bake in a 375° oven for about 10 to 15 minutes. When light to the touch, and the cake pulls away from the sides of the pan, it is done. Cool thoroughly. Put the layers together with whipped cream. Top with more whipped cream, and cover the top with chopped and whole nuts.

Here is the final gazebo with beautiful plantings. When my mother passed away she left an insurance policy. We boys used the money to build this and the large gazebo in her honor in front of Ashleigh's Boutique. I hope she's proud of it. I'm sure she is. Her marriage to Dad of 54 years couldn't be better served than by using her money for the start of other young couples' lives together in this pair of wedding gazebos.

The Settlement today as photographed by our resident photo historian, Mr. Frank Flynn. Here, you see his wife, Marilyn, looking at something new no doubt. This book would not be nearly as complete without some of Frank's hundreds of photos of our growth. Thanks loads, Frank. Keep the pictures coming.

1999, we finally have street lights like years gone by. We paved $50,000 worth of parking lots and poured $50,000 worth of concrete sidewalks to help ensure a safer time while wandering around Patti's. A friend recently told me he thought it was expensive to eat at Patti's and I told him—"You get yummy food and excellent service in an ambiance like none other. Without charging any more than comparable chain restaurants, we provide as comforting a spiritual experience as we can. Patti's is so much more than a restaurant. Patti's is where memories are made, every day and with every trip." We do our very best to hold down expenses while providing you with the best experience we can and at the same time, provide growth opportunities for our employees and for the town. We're not perfect, but I like to think we're darned good, what do y'all think?

In 1977 when we first opened Patti's, a restaurant called The Iron Kettle was thriving just down the street. People would be wrapped around the porches at The Kettle when we wouldn't have a person to serve in our place. Over the years, we developed a following and The Iron Kettle fell on hard times. In 1998, after being closed and purchased by our family, The Iron Kettle reopened. We reinvigorated the place with the spirit of its heyday. Today, The Kettle is a huge success with many of our guests visiting both Patti's and The Iron Kettle. The Kettle features good old home style cooking very similar to the original recipes Mom started Patti's with.

Shorty, Jan and Rosa are still there after many, many years to make sure the flavor of the Kettle's history isn't lost and today, Deannie Norman and Darnell Moneymaker are your managers. They welcome you back to take a walk into the original part of Thomas Lawson's Boston Block still standing underneath all the cedar siding. Grand Rivers' history has come full circle.

1999, before we started phase two of Patti's 1880's Settlement, the memorial gardens and chapel.

Time can and still does sometimes stand still in Grand Rivers. When I first moved to town there was this lovely, fun lady named Miss Linda Ray who, with her husband Tommy, operated the business across the street from Hamburger Patti's. She called her establishment, Linda Ray's BBQ and Antiques. Linda is one of my best supporters and I hers. In 1994, the Buchanon family (Frank is our mayor presently and has been for some time now), Frank, Marilyn and Matthew, sold us the property that you see here. It was a huge favor because we now could fix up the street in front of Patti's. Before I go on I'd like to say that Linda is still here in her antique store very nearly every day of the year. She is the most colorful person in Grand Rivers. She's our resident story-teller. She's our workhorse during festivals. She's a great (and interesting) lady to know. I can't begin to devote enough space in this book to justify what she has done for me and our town over our 24 years of knowing each other. I'll never forget when there weren't very many people who'd talk to me and she would sit and stitch her quilt tops and we'd gossip for hours. Today life moves too quickly but every time I have a few minutes I walk over and get a dose of her love, a pitcher that will never be empty and I thank God for that and for her.

Here, next to Linda's is part of phase two in Patti's development. This is the new home of Sew Cool Embroidery and Gifts owned by the lovely Laurie McWilliams, one of our past gift shop managers. This new building is also home to Anna's Emporium which is named after Michael T.'s and Lawana's youngest daughter and middle child. On the main street, we are trying to put back structures much like those Thomas Lawson had built while he was here. Unfortunately because of economic hard times, not one of the many commercial buildings that stood in 1900 in Grand Rivers stands today. They were either torn down, fell down or burned down.

Notice Linda Ray's antique shop to the left.

278

I'd like to personally thank the Buchanon family, if I might, for selling us this land. They are the most successful people in town and surely didn't need the cash. They are just so generous and kind to all of us here in our little city. They are an example of people who live by the golden rule. I admire and respect them greatly. Marilyn is a jewel who truly is a friend to Patti's. She is presently working on the development of our jetty where she will be able to use her abundant and valuable talents and strengths to ensure this project is completed beautifully and enduringly for all our residents and visitors to enjoy.

Her husband is the mayor and for the privilege of having this often thankless job, he is paid the royal sum of $1 per year. He has the patience of a saint and won a huge landslide victory in his last reelection. We all think the world of this family and let us suffice it to say that without their support in selling us two parcels of land, Patti's would not include much of what you can experience today. These parcels have proven crucial to the development of our Settlement. They are the land that Mr. Bill's and the Settlement sits on as well as the land across the street. Patti's Settlement and Grand Rivers would not be on the great climb upward that it is presently on if they weren't kind enough to part with these pieces of property. Thanks to you both for being so good to my family. You will always be special in our hearts. You are a huge part of our history and hopefully will be big in our future as well.

Marilyn, Frank and Matthew Buchanon—role models for all of us in knowing how to live a good, community spirited life. Miss Jean Reed, you're awfully special as well. Thanks for your bringing Marilyn into the world and for raising her and David to be such sweet people. Dottie, Margie and I sure do love the goodies you bring.

Folks, in my next book, I'm going to tell more stories about the history of the people who are Grand Rivers' past, present and future, so look for it.

We've had more trouble making this store work than any of the others and I'm not quite sure why. First it was an ice cream and sandwich shop which people loved but the season was too short. Financially, it just wouldn't work. Then we tried Anna's Closet, a children's store. It was a small version of a Disney store but we couldn't buy clothes as cheaply as Walmart was selling them. We tried for two years but Anna's failed also. This year, 2000, we are putting in Anna's Emporium, a family and men's store with more gift items. I think I finally have the right people and right gift lines. Maybe Anna, a little older now, will even come help with the store. If you see her, don't forget to say hi. She's the shy one in the family, at least when she first meets you.

The Miss Carrie Rhodes house (the Ross family homestead from the turn of the century) has been empty for at least 24 years. Our family was able to buy the property about 6 years ago and it remained as shown here until early 1999 when God sent Miss Cathy Tyree to us. This absolutely smashing lady and her family (husband, Dan; daughter, Amie; son-in-law, Doug Parham and grandson, Marcus) fell in love, literally, with this old house. Cathy has two other stores, one in downtown Paducah and the other in Governor's Square Mall in Clarksville, TN. She wanted to move to Small Town, USA. I could barely believe it. I had talked with our fire department about burning the old house down on several occasions but couldn't bring myself to destroy something of such historic value when there just isn't much remaining to remind us of Grand Rivers' very, very interesting past. Luckily, Cathy and I worked out a deal on renting the old house and she and her whole family brought in friends and the work began. The old derelict structure regained some of its grand appearance. At least it was cleaned up and spruced up.

Here you see the Rhodes/Ross house before Cathy started work—the fall of 1998.

1999 was Cathy's first year in business and one day I went to visit. She told me she did more business in her Grand Rivers store than in either of her mall stores over her first four months of being open. I literally jumped for joy. I thought, 'Praise the Lord', finally I may have an angel who can go out and spread the word about our little town and help me attract other special people to come and help make our town grow. Hopefully, we will continue to compete in this hard world of retail. Folks, when you see the Dawahare's family bring a store to town, you'll know I finally feel successful in this quest. Keep an eye on us and Grand Rivers. I haven't been able to convince them yet, but I never give up.

Perseverance is one of my greatest strengths. I guess I learned it from the story book Mother read to me when I was little about Tootle, the little train that could. If I believe it, it can happen. I'll make it happen. So watch for a Dawahare's—just for fun, watch. Cathy and family, your personality and your unconditionally loving heart is such a bright spot in my life. May your family and its future grow stronger within the relationship of our family for many years to come. Welcome to Grand Rivers, girl-friend.

In the spring of 1999, the Tullar family bought the Ridgetop Mall. When we first moved to town, the property belonged to Mary Knoth. When her husband passed away, it became too much for her. Julia and Chet Badger bought the property. At that time, there were seven little fishing cottages that rented very cheaply. Julia and Chet came in and spent a great deal of money building brand new buildings, renovating the others and laying out the gardens and pathways that became the Ridgetop Mall. It too was a retail shopping mall. Unfortunately, investment money alone can't keep Grand Rivers afloat and the mall became a victim of the big malls and huge wholesale stores.

This mall has been mostly empty with the exception of the new Lite Side Café owned by Bob and Irene Bryan, Unique Nautiques owned by Sherri Bernard and her mom, Janice Breedlove, and a folk art workshop owned by Pat Moore and her daughter, Nickie. Pat is a long-time friend of ours who opened the very first addition to Hamburger Patti's in the late 70's, The Owl's Roost. She is converting half her building into a gallery of her handiwork this spring and it will be called, Uncommon Gallery. We hopefully will have the other stores rented in the next couple of months or by the time this book is published. My family has already gone in and spent a lot of money to fix the place up again. Michael T. has lots of beautiful plants to add this year and Lonnie and crew have been pouring additional concrete walks and driveways and the most impressive retaining wall Grand Rivers has ever seen. Hopefully, we can turn the mall around so there will be more for everybody to do in town once they get here.

Ladies and gentlemen, this is the Thomas Lawson/Tullar house. This is the original condition it was in when Mike and I bought it. The house had been empty for fifteen years. It was tied up in an estate disagreement over ownership and one person wouldn't consent to sell the house. He said it could rot down before he'd consent to sell it. It's a long story I'll share another time, but he had some justification for his stance. Let me suffice it to say—when I first came to town I tried to buy an old house that had been empty for 10 years. The very next day it sold to Mabel Nash who had managed the Iron Kettle for many years. I was very disappointed but that was my first lesson in small town politics. Outsiders often don't find acceptance comes easily. Three weeks later, Mom and I went all the way to St. Louis to talk with the heir to another empty house 2 doors down from the one you see above. It too had been built by Thomas Lawson and it too had been vacant for 15 years and was a complete wreck. The lady agreed to sell it to Mom and me. This was on a Sunday. We said we'd get the papers drawn up Monday. Monday afternoon, her son sold the house to someone else, DANG— this was becoming the pits.

I had almost decided to say 'heck with this town' when I read this book called "On Top of the Mountain" by Samuel Goldwin of MGM fame. In it he stated that when life gets you down so much you should just get down on your knees and pray. He felt that God would hear your prayers. He said to pray to God to hold you, to carry you for a while if need be and to turn yourself and your life over to him to manage for a while. I remembered my walk on the beach back in 1975 when I was at my wit's end.

I'd been talking to the Jolly heirs for almost 3 months. I'd always loved the house. I got down on my knees that night after reading the book and asked the

Lord to help me. I cried and told him to please help me figure out what it is he wants me to do. May God be my witness, the phone rang at 8:00 the next morning. Mom and Edna Hooks, our first employee and present day owner of the Grand Rivers Fish Market, were swinging on the front porch of the motel. Mom and Dad lived in one of the six units and I lived in another. Michael Lee was still in California. Mom came to my room and told me I had a phone call. It was Roy Jolly, the reticent heir. He told me he'd decided to sell. Even today, as I sit here and write this story, I get goose bumps—some twenty-three years later. It was God's will being done. God had worked another miracle in my life. He wanted me in Grand Rivers. He wanted Mike and me to have our house. The grand old lady of Grand Rivers is still our house and we give her all the love money can afford. She's our family, the Tullar family's home. She's the image of Thomas Lawson and his dream that Grand Rivers would be his Boston of the west. Well, maybe we'll never be the Boston of the west—but we certainly are a little town in middle America where everybody knows each other's name and a whole bunch more about each other. We'll no doubt want to know all about you and your family when you decide to make Grand Rivers home. It's a terrific place to visit, live, work and play.

Thomas Lawson/Tullar home circa 1989. It has since gone through a major renovation (in 1998 and 1999) which will be outlined in our next book.

When Dad first came to Grand Rivers in 1975, he stayed at the Belair Motel across KY Lake in Marshall County, then owned by two wonderful people, Walt and Olga Edwards. He tells me how they recommended that he eat at the Iron Kettle restaurant in Grand Rivers. So he drove over to the Kettle

Lake living at its best.

and fell in love with the little town—remember, back then over ⅓ of the town's commercial district was boarded up and derelict. Then, there were two bait shops, two gas stations, two motels and the grocery store and that was very nearly it.

Coconut Crunch Pie

4 egg whites	1 cup graham cracker crumbs
Pinch of salt	½ cup coconut
1 cup sugar	½ cup pecans
1 teaspoon vanilla	

Beat egg whites at high speed of electric mixer until stiff. Add salt, gradually add sugar and fold in vanilla. Stir in graham cracker crumbs, coconut, and pecans. Pour into a well-buttered pie pan and bake at 350° for 20 minutes.

Serve with whipped cream or sliced bananas and whipped cream.

Anyway, Mrs. Nash, the manager of the Iron Kettle, owned the Grand Rivers Motel at the time and rented Dad the little two bedroom cottage which later became Grandmother's house. Dad fell in love with the area and brought Mom up from Florida for a look. Well, she wasn't thrilled at first but she began to meet some wonderful folks such as Linda Ray, Pat Moore, Doug and Alma Parrish and Brother Ellis from the Baptist church. She decided this was a nice place. To make a long story short, the Nash family sold the Motel to Mom and Dad and so goes the rest of the story. If Mable Nash hadn't sold the motel to us, I guess we wouldn't be here today.

The lakes are what Dad really fell in love with—remember, we lived in Hawaii, then Southern California, then Florida, then here. We, as a family, have always been near the water. Kentucky Lake and Lake Barkley make up the largest man-made bodies of water in the country. Dad realized the potential for this area. He realized the population was getting older and more people would be looking for areas to retire. He recognized that with Land Between the Lakes at our back door and being surrounded on three sides by water, our little town had vast potential. The leisure activities of houseboating, skiing, fishing, hunting, hiking, swimming, sailing and just relaxing were endless. So here we are. Today the year is 2000 in beautiful downtown Grand Rivers where every day is a new beginning for the rest of our lives.

FUN——why not take a little time out every once in a while and enjoy life? Our lakes are just the place to get together, meet new and old friends and relax and enjoy the life God blesses us all with. Remember, America is the land of opportunity. God gives us the possibility to make something of our lives. It's up to us if we want to make life good for ourselves and for others. I hope when all is said and done, our family has done more than its fair share to make life better for others.

Our area is blessed with great natural beauty. The rock quarry is a must see when visiting Kentucky Lake. The rock used to make Kentucky Dam in the late 30's and early 40's was taken from this site at the edge of the river and when the lake was formed, the quarry flooded. The water is over 100 feet deep with sheer, unobstructed walls which makes it ideal for thrill seekers who dive from the tops of those walls.

Here is another story illustrating how hard work and being smart enough can pay off with personal and professional success. This is Lighthouse Landing also known as Kentucky Lake Sails and this transformation happened right here in Grand Rivers. I'll share more about this story in my next book on Grand Rivers but let me say that Marty and Brenda Colburn have accomplished every bit as much as my family has and in the next couple of years, the two families and their respective businesses will grow closer and closer together. My dad has had one immensely strong dream for Grand Rivers. He wanted a jetty system built at the lakefront where folks from all over the lakes could come and tie up their boats and walk into town. Grand Rivers is the only city on the lakes and has the greatest opportunity to become a destination for all boaters. Green Turtle Bay and Kentucky Lake Sails are always full so we need dockage for transient traffic solely. Kentucky Lake, together with Lake Barkley, represent the largest inland sailing waters in America excluding the Great Lakes. Our beach is pictured just over the sailboats.

One of the purposes of our jetty development is to attract the Delta Queen and Mississippi Queen and their many guests to stop as they pass by Grand Rivers. The jetty was started years ago but recently we received a grant for $292,000 to further develop this asset.

Here is our beach and jetty, circa 1999. We are hoping for further development and expansion to build a waterfront facility like none other in the area. We hope to have docks on this jetty and we hope to build a lighthouse on the jetty's furthest point into the lake so we can say our beacon of hospitality reaches out to everyone who passes our way. I hope Dad's dream becomes a reality. It's the best thing in the world for our city.

Here I stand before you at The Kapok Tree restaurant in Clearwater, Florida. It and the following picture are a reminder of what once was. I know if I forget who my customers are and forget that our customers come first, there won't be a Patti's someday, just like there isn't a Kapok Tree today. Life in the business world, just as in the human realm is tenuous at best. The dedication to quality of our employees; great food, impeccable service, warm smiles, helpful personalities and the spirits of good people have made Patti's what you experience there today. These things must be guarded and I'm aware of this.

Michael T., Lawana, Arielle, Anna, Adam, Anita, Marian and all the extended family that makes up the Tullar family in the year 2000 and beyond; be proud of what you individually and collectively have accomplished. Be careful not to gloat, for what the Lord giveth, the Lord can take away. As long as you all realize as I did when I first hitch hiked into this town to visit Mom and Dad in the 70's that the Lord wants us working here. He wants us to build a place where people can forget their worries and be closer to Him for a short while in surroundings filled with good food, beautiful gardens, happy people and love.

I hope and think we have done God's work fairly well. It is my wish that you all nurture this spirit among your employees and guests in order to build on this foundation left to us by Mom and Dad. I'm sitting next to a beautiful and relaxing pool in Florida (Mike and Charlie's house there) writing this and I know Mom's here guiding my hand as I write this. I feel her presence. I hope and pray that I've made her and Dad proud. I hope your legacy is preserved through this book as Mom's was in the first cookbook. I love you both, for who you have been as parents and for who you've been as friends. Thanks for making me your son and for accepting the in-laws, Wilfred, Michael Lee and Lawana into the family with open arms.

The Kapok Tree Restaurant — Clearwater, Florida at its height.

May 15, 2000

Dad passed away on Monday, the 15th of May at 11:05 just five minutes after he finished watching his Price is Right T.V. show, the day after Mother's Day which would have been Mom and Dad's 56th Wedding Anniversary. (You see, Dad said they got married on Mother's Day 56 years ago.) He told me the Tuesday before he died he was tired and ready to go. It truly was his time — we as a family hereby close a chapter in the lives of two exceptional people — our parents.

It has been our family's upbringing to celebrate this event because our faith in God and in heaven is so strong. There is no doubt in my mind Mom reached down and grabbed ahold of her husband's hand and carried him to heaven with her. I told Dad the day before that he'd better pack his bags because Mom's going to plan on doing lots of traveling and his health wasn't going to slow him down any longer, no more excuses — a traveling he was a-going.

Here I am just as Dad requested with Father Sanus Doyle presiding over Dad's Memorial Service which we had in our garden's gazebo. As you can see Dad's in the plaster of Paris pig the lovely Pat Long made for him to reside in and Mom's in her teapot, surrounded by the families' pictures, lots of flowers and wonderful friends.

I did something very different at Dad's services I've never seen done before, but heck, people expect me to be different, creative. Susie and Stella (Dad's girls) combined some of Mom's ashes with some of Dad's ashes and put them into soufflé cups and I explained that anybody who would like to take a part of Mom & Dad with them, please be my guest. One couple was going to take Mom & Dad in an airplane and spread their ashes over Patti's Settlement; one couple was going out on the lake fishing and taking Mom & Dad out with them. Mom's still fishing for that "catch of the day." The Flynns took Mom & Dad to the Church Memorial Gardens; and my sister took two cups back to California to share with her family at their homes. Before you knew, all thirty-five cups were gone and people were asking if there were any more. I felt sorry to say no, there weren't any more but the love I felt from all these friends was beyond my wildest belief. Maybe a new tradition has been born. Thanks again to Mom & Dad!

Being raised in the Episcopal faith, communion has always been part of our heritage. I believe just as Jesus had broken bread just before He died, we too have it with our final blessing. I chose to use Mom's flower pot bread that Joann (the baker) made special for Dad as she has for so many of Patti's friends. It, too, made Dad's service very personal.

Linda probably will miss Dad and Calvin Swine the most — it was Linda's antique shop across from Patti's where Dad & Calvin Swine stopped every day for treats and talk. This picture in my mind will never go away; it is a picture of past Grand Rivers when cars were so few that they stopped regularly for the old man in his Hee-Haw overalls walking his pig, Calvin, only to have the kids shout "Look at that funny dog." In return, Dad would laugh and say "I think my dog/pig is pretty." Linda had this wonderful pig made in Dad's honor — love to you always, Miss Ray.

Cindy and her mom, Alice Coleman of C & A Christmas Exchange, have been a huge part of Patti's 1880's Settlement for many years. Their tireless efforts to run a retail store is beyond compare. Here they are pictured at the reception at Mom and Dad's house. Dad loved you ladies so much and the goats too!

Here's Dottie, our retail manager (left), and Miss Pat Moore (center), the original retail shop owner of the "Owl's Roost Gift Shop" (which was pictured earlier). Miss Pat Moore was the owner of our very first addition to Hamburger Patti's Ice Cream Parlor. On the right is Roni, my sister. They are in front of a stained glass window at Mom and Dad's house. Notice the smiles on everyone's faces — death is something we celebrate — thanks to God.

These two ladies spent the last years taking care of Mom and then Dad so they never had to go to a nursing home. These ladies are truly two of God's greatest gifts to us mortals here on earth. They have so much love and compassion in their hearts; anyone who comes into their presence is automatically blessed. Today, they are taking care of me and helping Lawana take care of the grandkids and, most importantly, they're taking care of Mom and Dad's house and two miniature pinchers, Elke and Sassy. When Mom first found out she was ill, she told me her greatest fear is what would happen to her girls. Dad took care of them till now, today they have Mary, Stella and Susie to love them everyday.

Folks, this is a happy ending to the most wonderful of stories, an American story we all can relate to in one way or another, a generation of history going good-bye. When marriage was a lifelong commitment, where friends took care of friends, and families were families. Where you could, at 50-plus years of age, start life all over again at the bottom and build your future into something *"OH SO SPECIAL,"* leaving behind memories for generations to come to remember and, most importantly of all, to leave smiling faces of your friends and family behind. Love, if you will, goes all around and around and around.

"Our Future"

Today in our town of 350 people, we have a committed mayor, the Honorable Frank Buchanon, a strong city council, an Economic Development Foundation, a 1% tax on restaurants to help build the city's infrastructure, a vibrant Chamber of Commerce, and outstanding volunteers throughout our community. All working together to make Grand Rivers a showcase of God's love for all who come to enjoy. Our future is bright with the kids who are the employees of Patti's today and who are the company's future. Arielle, Anna, Adam: I hope you will treasure these memories that have been saved for you and you, someday, will build upon them with love in your hearts for all who have made this story possible.

Thank you,

Thank you, everyone.

This is one American family's story.

Index

Mail to: *Patti's 1880's Settlement*
Attn: Gift Shop
P.O. Box 111
Grand Rivers, KY 42045
www.pattis_settlement.com

For orders, call: 270-362-8844   Fax 270-362-7314

Discover, Visa & MasterCard accepted

Credit Card #_____ Exp. Date_____

Please send me:
_____copies of ***Miss Patti's Cookbook***   @ $17.95 each _____

_____copies of ***Grace of Patti's Cookbook*** @ $19.95 each _____

Postage and handling $3.50 _____

KY residents add 6% sales tax $1.08 each _____

Patti's Specialty Items

Patti's Pork Chop Seasonings, 10 oz. bottle . . . . . . $6.99 _____

Patti's Pork Chop Sauce, 13 oz. bottle . . . . $6.99 _____

Patti's BBQ Sauce, 13 oz. bottle . . . . $3.99 _____

Patti's Homemade
Strawberry Butter, 12 oz. jar . . . . $4.99 _____

Patti's Preserves, Jams and Jellies . . . . $2.69 to $4.69 _____

Patti's Homemade Loaf Bread
2 lb. Loaf . . . . $2.99 _____

Patti's Homemade Pies
Sawdust Pie, Boo Boo Pie . . . . $7.99 _____
Chocolate Chip Pecan Pie $7.99
Butterscotch Chip Pecan Pie $7.99

TOTAL _____

6% State sales tax and shipping will be added to each order. (KY checks only)

Make checks payable to ***Patti's 1880's Settlement***

Ship to:

_____

_____

_____